MANAGEMENT VS. THE UNIONS

MANAGEMENT

VS.

THE UNIONS

How to Win

EDWARD F. MURPHY

𝔰𝔡

STEIN AND DAY/*Publishers*/New York

First published in 1971
Copyright © 1971 by Edward F. Murphy
Library of Congress Catalog Card No. 70–163497
All rights reserved
Published simultaneously in Canada by Saunders of Toronto Ltd.
Designed by David Miller
Printed in the United States of America
Stein and Day/*Publishers*/7 East 48 Street, New York, N. Y. 10017
ISBN 0–8128–1420–7

To darling Maggie

CONTENTS

INTRODUCTION   9
1 What the National Labor Relations Act
  Provides—in Everyday Language   13
2 Can Your Company Be Hauled Before the NLRB?   23
3 A Company Doesn't Have to Have a Union to
  Run into "Union Trouble"   27
4 How the NLRB Operates   31
5 Why the Right "Appropriate Unit"
  Can Help You Win   43
6 How to Keep a Union out of Your Plant   47
7 How to Win When a Union Organizer
  Makes Your Plant His Target   53
8 How the Employees' Representative Is
  Chosen Normally   65
9 Union Security Agreements   69
10 How to Avoid the Employer's Five Cardinal Sins   75
11 Some Things You Can Prevent Unions from Doing   93
12 How to Avoid Bargaining with a Union
   Your Employees Don't Want   101
13 Boycotting—What It Is and How to Deal with It   109
14 The Law of the Collective-Bargaining Game   115
15 How to Avoid Bargaining about Your
   Business Decisions   125
16 Management vs. Strikers   131
17 What to Watch out for When the Union
   Calls Off an Economic Strike   145
18 Protecting Your Employee from His Union's Wrath   153

CONTENTS

19 How to Win by Using the Lockout   167
20 You May Buy a Union Contract and a Union
    When You Buy a Business   171
21 When May a Union Hurt Your Retail Store by
    Picketing or Handbilling?   175
22 How to Withdraw from a Multi-Employer
    Bargaining Unit   177
23 When Must You Let an Outsider Decide
    Employee Grievances?   179
24 How to Present a Case to an Arbitrator
    Yourself—and Win   183

INTRODUCTION

THE SUREST WAY for management to avoid the financial blows and mortification which follow violation of the National Labor Relations Act is to have some knowledge of the fundamentals of that Act. It is amazing how few members of management have that knowledge even though the Act has been on the books for over thirty-five years.

In January 1971 Edward B. Miller, chairman of the National Labor Relations Board (NLRB), made a speech at Louisiana State University. He noted that he had been in office a bit over six months, and went on to say:

> A phenomenon which came as something of a surprise to me as a newcomer to the Board was the astonishingly high recurrence of what might be called classic cases of the 8(a)(1) and 8(a)(3) variety which continue to clog the Board's calendars.

> After 35 years during which there has been a law prohibiting employer interference with employees' rights to self-organization and self-determination and prohibiting the discharge or discipline of employees engaged in prounion or antiunion activity, it would have seemed reasonable to assume that employers across the land would, by now, have accommodated themselves to at least these basic principles of law.

> But there are still apparently a very substantial number of employers who have either not had enough exposure to organizational activity among their employees so as to have become familiar with our Act or who are in that small minority of employers who choose deliberately to disregard employee rights. So there continues the dreary parade of 8(a)(1) and 8(a)(3) cases, most of them not posing any new or difficult questions of interpretation, but instead where the record contains clear, unmistakable evidence of classic violations—threats to close the plant

9

because of union activity, direct promises of improved wages and working conditions if only the employees will vote against the union, discharges and threats of discharge of employees who take an active part in organizational efforts, and all of the other typical acts and statements which even a beginning student of labor law would recognize as a violation of the Act.

This phenomenon suggests to me that there is still a real need for the labor bench and bar to continue our efforts to educate the business community as to the basic framework of federal labor law. Many bar associations and many employer associations have made a major contribution in this area by publishing easy-to-read brochures and by conducting educational sessions periodically so that businessmen may be informed as to the fundamental tenets of our law. I had begun to think, before coming to Washington, that perhaps these efforts were no longer necessary. I now know that this is not true. I would therefore urge the continuation of these efforts, so that in time we may be able to diminish, by preventive education, much unnecessary conflict and needless litigation in this area.

It must always be remembered that the National Labor Relations Act, when passed on July 5, 1935, was partisan legislation. Until the Act was amended by the Taft-Hartley Act in 1947, it was aimed solely at management. Five types of employer conduct were banned; no activities by unions were condemned. Although the balance was restored somewhat by the Taft-Hartley Act, which condemned certain activities of unions, the Labor Act is still worded in such general terms that it can be construed by the National Labor Relations Board, which administers it, in such a way that management is nearly always the loser. The Act says that it is the "policy of the United States" to encourage collective bargaining and union organization. But it also says that the policy of the United States is to protect the rights of individual employees in their relations with unions, including their right "to refrain" from joining or aiding a union. However, the NLRB during the Kennedy-Johnson years subordinated the rights of individual employees to the encouragement of unionism. In effect, the Act puts the full power of the national government behind the labor movement. Therefore, an employer must realize that, usually, when he is faced with organizational activities by a union or by his own employees or when he is charged with having committed an unfair labor practice, he already has at least one strike against him.

The employer and his foreman must gain a basic knowledge of the Act so that they will realize that when certain things happen— for example, an employee advocating a union—they may not react as a boss of forty years ago might have reacted. They must not act impulsively, or they might find themselves in hot water without even realizing how they got there. They must know when a Labor Act problem is probably present and consult a labor relations lawyer *before* they act, not after the damage has been done.

It is not the purpose of this book to teach employers labor relations law. Even a thousand-page casebook used in the law schools cannot do that, for the law which springs from the National Labor Relations Act is a dynamic, constantly growing body of rules concerning what employers, employees, and unions can and cannot do without violating the Act.

Attempts to generalize always run the risk of omitting all the little exceptions into which, for some strange reason, most cases seem to fit. And once the exceptions are stated, one ends with a legal treatise designed for lawyers rather than laymen. This book presents broad, general principles only. Countless subrules and minute exceptions to broad general principles are not included.

The main purpose of the book is to alert you to the possible presence of a problem under the Labor Act and to caution you to use restraint until you have received professional advice. As former National Labor Relations Board general counsel Stuart Rothman has said, "Long experience under the Labor Act has taught that when parties fully understand their rights and obligations, they are more ready and able to adjust their differences voluntarily. Seldom does a man go into a courtroom, a hearing, or any other avoidable contest, knowing that he is in the wrong and that he can expect to lose the decision. No one really likes to be publicly recorded as a law violator (and a loser too!)."

The consequences of ignorance of the Labor Act—time-consuming and costly as they are and often followed by bitterness and antagonism—can be avoided if you have a basic understanding of the provisions of the Act. If you recognize when you need expert assistance, this book will have achieved its purpose.

1

WHAT THE NATIONAL LABOR RELATIONS ACT PROVIDES—IN EVERYDAY LANGUAGE

THE NATIONAL LABOR Relations Act is composed of the original Act passed in 1934 (sometimes called the Wagner Act after its sponsor, Senator Robert F. Wagner), as amended by the Taft-Hartley Act in 1945 and the Landrum Griffin Act in 1959. Here's what the Act says in everyday language:

Section 1 states that the policy of the United States is to encourage collective bargaining and protect the rights of employees and the public.

Section 2 defines terms used in the Labor Act. The most important are the definitions of the words "employee," "supervisor," and "employer."

The term "employee" includes workers out on strike but excludes any individual:

Employed as an agricultural laborer

In domestic service

Employed by parent or spouse

Having the status of an independent contractor

Employed as a supervisor

Employed by an employer subject to the Railway Labor Act (airlines as well as railroads)

Employed by the United States Government or any wholly owned government corporation or any Federal Reserve Bank, or any state or political subdivision thereof such as a city, town, or school district.

Employed by hospitals operated entirely on a nonprofit basis

Supervisors are excluded from the definition of "employee" and therefore are not covered by the Act. Whether an individual is a

13

supervisor for purposes of the Labor Act depends on his authority over employees and not merely his title. A supervisor is defined by the Act as any individual who, acting in the interest of his employer, has the authority to cause another employee to be hired, transferred, suspended, laid off, recalled, promoted, discharged, assigned, rewarded, or disciplined, either by taking the action himself or by recommending it to a superior; or who has the authority to direct other employees or adjust their grievances; provided, in all cases, that the exercise of authority is not of a merely routine or clerical nature but requires the exercise of independent judgment. For example, a foreman who determined which employees would be laid off after the job superintendent directed him to lay off four employees would be considered a supervisor and would not be covered by the Act; a "strawboss" who, after someone else determined which employees would be laid off, merely informed the employees of the layoff and who neither directed other employees nor adjusted their grievances would not be considered a supervisor and would be covered by the Act.

The term "employer" includes any person who acts as an agent of an employer, but it does *not* include the following: the federal government or any state government, or any political subdivision of either, or any government corporation or Federal Reserve Bank; hospitals operated entirely on a nonprofit basis; any employer subject to the Railway Labor Act.

Sections 3, 4, 5, and 6 create the National Labor Relations Board and the Office of General Counsel and deal with their salaries, duties, powers, etc. The NLRB includes the Board itself, which is composed of five members with their respective staffs, the General Counsel of the NLRB and his staff, and the NLRB Regional Offices. The General Counsel has final authority on behalf of the Board in respect to the investigation of charges and issuance of complaints. The Board members and the General Counsel are appointed by the President, with consent of the Senate. The Board members serve five-year terms and the General Counsel, four years. Headquarters of the Board and the General Counsel are in

Washington, D.C. To assist in administering and enforcing the law, the NLRB has established thirty-one regional offices and a number of other field offices. These offices, located in major cities throughout the nation, are under the general supervision of the General Counsel.

Section 7 guarantees to employees the right to unionize, engage in collective bargaining, and participate in other concerted activities (group activities) for their mutual protection. It also guarantees employees the right to refrain from doing any of these things except as such right may be vetoed by an agreement requiring membership in a union as a condition of keeping a job as authorized in Section 8(a)(3).

Section 8(a)(1) says it is against the law (an unfair labor practice, it's called) for an employer to try to do anything that interferes with the exercise by employees of their Section 7 rights.

Section 8(a)(2) says it is against the law for an employer to dominate a union or give it financial or other aid. But an employee may confer with the employer concerning a grievance during working hours without loss of pay.

Section 8(a)(3) says it is illegal for an employer to discriminate with respect to hiring or terms of employment in order to encourage or discourage membership in a union. But it contains an exception as far as encouraging membership in a union is concerned: it permits any employer to discharge an employee who fails to pay union initiation fees and dues under a lawful agreement requiring union membership as a condition of keeping the job (a union-shop agreement). But an employer cannot justify discharging an employee even under such an agreement if he has reason to believe that membership in the union was not open to the employee on the same terms as apply to others or that the employee was denied membership in the union for some reason other than failure to pay regular dues and the initiation fee.

Section 8(a)(4) says it is against the law for an employer to discharge an employee because he has filed charges against the employer with the NLRB or given testimony in a matter arising under the Labor Act.

Section 8(a)(5) says it is against the law for an employer to refuse to bargain with the union.

Section 8(b)(1)(A) says it is against the law for a union to do anything that interferes with the exercise by the employees of their Section 7 rights. This ban is not intended to interfere with a union's right to prescribe its own rules concerning membership.

Section 8(b)(1)(B) says it is against the law for a union to interfere with an employer's right to pick his own bargaining representative.

Section 8(b)(2) says it is against the law for a union to solicit an employer to discriminate against an employee in violation of Section 8(a)(3) above.

Section 8(b)(3) says it is against the law for a union to refuse to bargain with the employer (the other side of Section 8(a)(5) above).

Section 8(b)(4) prohibits a union from inducing any employee to strike or threatening any employer to accomplish objects A, B, C, or D below:

Object A: to compel an employer or self-employed person to join any union or employer organization or to force an employer to enter a "hot cargo" agreement defined by Section 8(e). Under Section 8(e) it is against the law for an employer and a union to make an agreement whereby the employer agrees to stop handling the product of or to stop doing business with any other employer. It also makes such an agreement void.

Object B: to put pressure on Company X so that it stops doing business with Company Y, with which the union has its real dispute.

Object C: to force an employer to bargain with a union other than the one that currently carries the NLRB's seal of approval (i.e., the one that the NLRB has "certified" as the representative of the employees involved).

Object D: to force an employer to assign certain work to employees who are members of one union rather than another.

The final provision in Section 8(b)(4) provides that nothing in said Section shall be construed "to prohibit publicity, other than picketing, for the purpose of truthfully advising the public, including consumers and members of a labor organization, that a product or products are produced by an employer with whom the labor organization has a primary dispute and are distributed by another employer." Such publicity is not protected, however, if it has "an effect of inducing any individual employed by any person other than the primary employer" to refuse to handle any goods or not to perform services.

Section 8(b)(5) says it is against the law for a union to demand an excessive initiation fee from employees who are subject to an agreement whereby they must join the union to keep their jobs (a union-shop agreement).

Section 8(b)(6) forbids a union to cause an employer to pay for services not performed or not to be performed ("featherbedding," it's called).

Section 8(b)(7) prohibits a union that is not currently certified as the employees' representative from picketing or threatening to picket with the object of obtaining recognition by the employer or acceptance by his employees as their representative. This is called "blackmail picketing." The object of picketing is ascertained from all the surrounding facts, including the messages on the picket signs and any communications between the union and the employer.

Blackmail picketing is prohibited in three specific instances: When the employer has lawfully recognized another union and there is a valid contract between them [8(b)(7)(A)]; when a valid NLRB representation election has been held within the previous twelve months (and, of course, the employees voted against the union); or when a representation petition is not filed by the union within a reasonable period of time, not to exceed thirty days from the commencement of such picketing. This last restriction is subject to an exception, which permits picketing to advise the public that an employer does not employ union members or have a contract with a union—so long as the pickets don't rouse in the bosoms of truck drivers an urge to respect the hoary union maxim: never cross a picket line. [8(b)(7)(C)]

If an 8(b)(7)(C) charge is filed against the picketing union and a representation petition is filed within a reasonable time after the picketing starts, a "quickie" election is held. (An ordinary election is held only after the Board has conducted a hearing and has determined that enough employees want the union so that an election will not be a futile expenditure of your tax dollars.)

Section 8(f) contains provisions relaxing the requirements for a valid union shop to exist in the construction industry.

Section 9(a) says that the union selected by the majority of employees in a unit appropriate for the purposes of collective bargaining shall be the *exclusive* representative of all the employees in the unit. An appropriate unit is a group of two or more employees who share *common employment and interests and conditions* and may reasonably be grouped together for purposes of collective bargaining. The determination of what is an appropriate unit is left to the discretion of the NLRB.

However, Section 9(b)(1) provides that the Board shall not approve as appropriate a unit that includes both professional and nonprofessional employees unless a majority of the professional employees vote to be included in the mixed unit.

Section 9(b)(3) prohibits the Board from including plant guards in the same unit with other employees.

Section 9(c)(1) authorizes the NLRB to hold elections to determine if employees wish to be represented by a union. It also allows the NLRB to hold an election to determine if the employees want to get rid of a union that has been representing them. This is called a "decertification election."

Section 9(c)(4) permits the union and the company to waive the hearing which is normally held by the Board before an election is ordered to determine such questions as whether enough employees are interested to make holding an election worthwhile.

Section 9(d) deals only with procedure when an NLRB order is appealed to one of the U.S. circuit courts of appeal. Strange as it may seem, the Board cannot enforce its own orders. The circuit courts must order a company or union to obey the Board's orders— or it may refuse to issue such an enforcement order.

Section 9(e) provides that if a company and a union have made a union-shop agreement pursuant to Section 8(a)(3) above, whereby employees must join the union to keep their jobs, 30 percent of the employees in the unit may file a petition saying they want to have the union stripped of the power to make such an agreement. When this happens the Board must hold an election on the question, and if a majority of employees in the unit vote in favor of the petition, the union-shop clause in the contract becomes a dead letter. This is called a "deauthorization election."

Section 10(a) empowers the Board to forbid companies and unions from committing "unfair labor practices."

Section 10(b) outlaws the filing of stale charges—those based on any unfair labor practices that happened more than six months previously.

Section 10(c) says that if the Board finds a union or company has committed an unfair labor practice, the Board may order it to "cease and desist" from such unfair labor practice and may take such other affirmative action, including reinstatement of employees with or without back pay, as will effectuate the policies of the Labor Act. This section contains a warning to the Board that it may not order the reinstatement of an employee who was discharged for cause.

Section 10(e) gives the Board the power to petition the U.S. Court of Appeals for a court decree enforcing the order of the Board if an employer or a union fails to comply with a Board order.

Section 10(f) provides that if any person is aggrieved by a final order of the Board granting or denying in whole or in part the relief sought, he may obtain a review of such order in any appropriate circuit court of appeals. When the court of appeals hears a petition concerning a Board order, it may enforce the order, remand it to the Board for reconsideration, change it, or set it aside entirely. If the court issues a decree enforcing the Board order, failure to comply may be punishable by fine or imprisonment for contempt of court.

In some cases the U.S. Supreme Court may be asked to review

the decision of a circuit court of appeals, particularly if there is a conflict in the views of different courts on the same important problem.

Section 10(g), (h), and (i) involve procedural matters.

Section 10(j) grants the Board the power to seek a temporary order from a federal district court enjoining a person from violating the Act whenever a complaint is filed that the person is doing so. This power is rarely exercised.

Section 10(k) provides an opportunity for parties charged with a violation of Section 8(b)(4)(D) (which prohibits a union from striking or inducing a strike to compel an employer to assign particular work to members of one union rather than another) to adjust their dispute during a ten-day period after notice of the 8(b)(4)(D) charge has been served. At the end of this period if the parties have not submitted to the Board satisfactory evidence that they have adjusted, or agreed on a method of adjusting the dispute, the Board must determine which of the competing groups is entitled to the work.

Section 10(l) gives priority to boycott and "blackmail picketing" cases. If a preliminary investigation shows that there is reasonable cause to believe that the charge is true and that a complaint should issue, Section 10(l) requires that a U.S. district court be petitioned to grant an injunction pending the final determination of the Board. The section authorizes the court to grant "such injunctive relief or temporary restraining order as it deems just and proper."

Section 13 guarantees the right to strike "except as specifically provided for" elsewhere in the Act. That is, the right to strike is not absolute.

Section 14(a) allows supervisors to join a union (but they don't get the protection of the Act because they are excluded from the definition of "employees").

Section 14(b) permits the states to pass laws forbidding union-shop contracts within their borders. These are called "right-to-work" laws.

Section 201 sets up the Federal Mediation and Conciliation Service, which tries to get companies and unions to reach agreements rather than to strike or lock out.

Section 206 sets up procedures for handling situations which in the opinion of the President could imperil the national health or safety.

Section 301(a) has turned out to be one of the most important sections of the Act because the Supreme Court has disregarded the apparent limitations of the words used by Congress and given its blessing to the creation of a new body of labor relations law. The one-sentence section reads: "Suits for violation of contracts between an employer and a labor organization representing employees in an industry affecting commerce as defined in this Act, or between labor organizations, may be brought in any district court of the United States having jurisdiction of the parties, without respect to the amount in controversy or without regard to the citizenship of the parties."

When the Act was first passed, everyone thought that all it meant was that, like a corporation, a union could be sued as an entity and that one did not have to serve a summons on every single union member.*

It was assumed to mean that it was not necessary that the parties be citizens of different states, the normal requirement for a federal district court to handle suits on contracts. To sum up— that it dealt solely with procedure. But the Supreme Court treated this sentence as granting revolutionary substantial rights and obligations quite beyond the literal meaning of the sentence. The Court held that this sentence meant that a court could order a company to submit a dispute to arbitration by a neutral third party if it had agreed to do so in a contract, and that a court could order a union not to strike in violation of its agreement in a contract not to strike.

Section 301(b) says that if a company gets a judgment for

---

* A union is an unincorporated association, and if one sues such an association he has to serve a summons on each member.

damages against a union it may be collected only from the assets of the union and not from the assets of the individual members of the union.

Section 302 makes it a crime for an employer to grease the palm of anyone representing his employees. However, it is lawful for an employer to turn over to a union money withheld from the wages of an employee as union dues so long as the employer holds a written assignment from the particular employee. This assignment cannot be irrevocable for a period of more than one year, or beyond the termination date of the applicable collective-bargaining agreement, whichever occurs sooner. This section also allows an employer to contribute to trust funds to provide pensions, life insurance, sick benefits, and the like so long as the employer and the union are equally represented in the administration of the funds.

Section 303 allows a company which has been injured by a secondary boycott or other activities banned in Section 8(b)(4) to sue the union for damages.

Section 305 bans strikes by government employees.

2

CAN YOUR COMPANY ~~stop~~
BE HAULED BEFORE THE NLRB?

THE NATIONAL LABOR Relations Board is not like a cop on the beat or the FBI. It has no authority to go out looking for violators of the Labor Act. A complainant must go to one of its regional offices and ask it to act.

The petitioner may ask the NLRB to hold an election to determine whether the employees at his company want to have a union represent them. This request is made on a form provided by the NLRB called a "petition." Or he may ask it to prevent his company from engaging in unfair labor practices. This request is made on a form, also provided by the NLRB, called a "charge."

The NLRB can go into action on a petition or a charge only if the company's business is one that "affects interstate commerce."

How do you know whether your company's business "affects interstate commerce"? The easiest way to find out is to ask yourself: "Does the company have to comply with the Wages and Hours Act? Does it have to pay employees the minimum hourly rate required by that law? Does it have to pay time and one-half for hours worked per week in excess of forty?"

If the answer is yes, then the business affects commerce. If the answer is no, you had better go see a lawyer right away to make sure that answer is right. Because darn few businesses today don't affect commerce. And if your company should be complying with the Wages and Hours Act, and isn't, brother you are in trouble!

Examples of enterprises "affecting commerce" would be: a manufacturing company in California that sells and ships its product to buyers in Oregon; a company in Georgia that buys supplies in Louisiana; a trucking company that transports goods from one point in New York State through Pennsylvania to another point in New York State; a radio station in Minnesota that has listeners in Wisconsin.

Although a company may not have any direct dealings with enterprises in any other state, its operations may nevertheless affect commerce. A Massachusetts manufacturing company that sells all of its goods to Massachusetts wholesalers affects commerce if the wholesalers ship to buyers in other states. The effects of a labor dispute involving the Massachusetts company would be felt in other states, and the labor dispute would therefore affect commerce. Using this test, you can see that the operations of almost any employer can be said to affect commerce. As a result, the authority of the NLRB could extend to all but purely local enterprises.

Let's assume your answer is yes, that your company does indeed affect commerce. That means the NLRB can start working on a petition or a charge someone has filed with it.

However, so many businesses affect commerce that the NLRB would be swamped if it bothered with all the small businesses that affect commerce. So it has set up some rules to distinguish the "small" from the "big." These are called "jurisdictional standards" and are based on the yearly amount of business done by the enterprise, or on the yearly amount of its sales or its purchases. They are stated in terms of total dollar volume of business and are different for different kinds of enterprises. Here are the principal standards in effect on March 1, 1971:

Nonretail business: Sales of goods to consumers in other states directly, or indirectly through others (called outflow), of at least $50,000 a year, or purchases of goods from suppliers in other states directly, or indirectly through others (called inflow), of at least $50,000 a year.

Retail enterprises: At least $500,000 total annual volume of business.

24

Office buildings and shopping centers: Total annual income of at least $100,000, of which $25,000 or more is paid by other organizations which meet any of the other standards except the indirect outflow and indirect inflow standards established for nonretail enterprises.

Public utilities: At least $250,000 total annual volume of business, or $50,000 direct or indirect outflow or inflow.

Newspapers: At least $200,000 total annual volume of business.

Radio, telegraph, television, and telephone businesses: At least $100,000 total annual volume of business.

Hotels, motels, and apartment houses: At least $500,000 total annual volume of business.

Privately owned hospitals and nursing homes operated for profit: At least $250,000 total annual volume of business for hospitals; at least $100,000 for nursing homes. Private hospitals which have no shareholders who would profit from their operation and public hospitals are excluded from NLRB jurisdiction by Section 2(2) of the Labor Act.

Taxicab companies: At least $500,000 total annual volume of business.

Transit systems: At least $250,000 total annual volume of business.

Transportation enterprises, links and channels of interstate commerce: At least $50,000 total annual income from furnishing interstate transportation service or performing services valued at $50,000 or more for enterprises that meet any of the standards except the indirect outflow and indirect inflow standards established for nonretail businesses.

Associations: Regarded as a single employer in that the annual business of all its members is totaled to determine whether any of the standards apply.

In the District of Columbia all businesses are subject to NLRB jurisdiction.

WARNING: Just because your company's business doesn't meet any of the above standards does not mean you can thumb your nose at the NLRB. The Board has established the policy that where an employer whose operations affect interstate commerce refuses to supply the Board with information concerning total annual business, etc., the Board may forget the standards and take the case against him.

3

A COMPANY DOESN'T HAVE TO HAVE A
UNION TO RUN INTO "UNION TROUBLE"

IT'S AMAZING HOW many employers don't know that they can be hauled before the NLRB for playing the role of the "boss" even though there's not a union within miles and even though their employees might be horrified at the very idea of being union members.

But that's the fact of the matter. The "boss" was killed off in 1935 by Congress when it passed the Wagner Act, under which employees are guaranteed by the federal government that they have the right to "engage in concerted activities for the purpose of mutual aid or protection."

The result is that if an employer fires or otherwise disciplines an employee who is engaged in "concerted activities" he may find himself hauled before the National Labor Relations Board and ordered to reinstate the discharged employee, give him the pay he would have earned if he had not been discharged, and further suffer the humiliation of having to post a notice—where all employees can read it—in effect confessing that he has sinned and promising to sin no more.

Here are a couple of examples:

The "us girls" case. Sandra Allison, to use one of a few fictitious names, was one of twelve office girls. They all worked the same hours and received the same salary. One was named Mickey. She was an exceptionally good stenographer and a very pretty girl with nice legs. One day Oscar Allworthy, the office manager, gave Mickey a raise—gave her *alone* a raise. As you might expect, she couldn't keep her mouth shut. She blabbed to the other girls.

27

The next morning during the coffee break, Sandra Allison and her co-workers Jean, Joan, Peggy, and Anita discussed Mickey's pay raise. They decided to talk to Allworthy and find out whether they too could expect a raise.

Sandra Allison walked up to Allworthy and said, "Us girls would like to talk to you this afternoon if you have any time."

"Sure," Allworthy replied.

But during the lunch hour Allworthy's assistant told him what the girls wanted to talk about. When Sandra returned from lunch a "temporary" was finishing the report Sandra had been typing during the morning. A summons came from Allworthy.

"You're fired, Sandra," growled Oscar Allworthy. "Go pick up your paycheck. And you can tell those girls out there that there isn't going to be any meeting this afternoon."

A few moments later a chalk-faced Sandra Allison was telling the girls in the steno pool of her fate.

"Why the mean old bastard," cried Mary Ann McCarthy. "We ought to have a union around here, that's what we ought to have."

There was no union around there. Never had been. There wasn't a union organizer within miles.

The next day Sandra went to the regional office of the National Labor Relations Board and filed a form charging the company with having committed an unfair labor practice. After investigation, a complaint was issued against the company, and the case eventually was heard before a trial examiner, in effect a judge. The company claimed that adverse economic conditions dictated a reduction in the size of its office staff. It also proved that Sandra was the worst typist of the group. But the trial examiner held that the NLRB's General Counsel had proved that the poor quality of Sandra's work was not the real reason why she had been fired. It was a mere pretext. After all, the company had put up with her for more than a year. The real reason why Sandra had been fired was that she had engaged in "concerted activity." She was not acting to win a raise for herself alone but for the other girls also; she was acting with respect to conditions of employment. The Labor Act guarantees that employees may act to improve their terms and conditions of employment. A boss who would discourage such activity will find he's bucking the power of the federal government. The company had to rehire Sandra and pay her the wages she had lost (Canteen Corporation, Case No. 13-CA-8414 [1968]).

The "chowder and marching society" case. A group of kids were working in a hamburger restaurant. After their employer changed his method of paying them, they held a meeting at the home of one of them to create an "organization."

One of the members of the "organization" told the manager about the meeting. The next day the manager assigned Gary Beckham, the leader of the "organization," to chop lettuce for use in the restaurant's specialty. Gary had never chopped lettuce before. Lettuce is properly chopped into cold water in order to preserve its crispness. Gary chopped half a crate of lettuce into water that was steaming hot. Along came the manager. Out on his ear went Gary.

In an opinion putting Gary back on the job with all the back pay he hadn't earned, the trial examiner said: "The company made much of the fact that the meeting smacked more of a chowder and marching society than an organization seriously dedicated to advancing the interests of its members as employees. But the fact that what transpired at the meeting may have had some of the farcical quality of a gathering of children to form a secret society is immaterial. The meeting was concerned with the grievances of the company's employees. Therefore I find that, when the charging parties [Gary and two of his pals] organized and conducted it, they were engaged in concerted activities for the purpose of mutual aid and assistance within the meaning of the Act" (*McDonald Carry-Out Restaurant*, Case No. 23-CA-3349 [1969]).

How to win. Avoid taking any kind of disciplinary action when a single employee raises a question concerning wages, hours, or working conditions affecting anyone other than himself alone. Use the old soft soap, but find out what the gripe is all about. Then try to satisfy the group grievance.

4

HOW THE NLRB OPERATES

THE NATIONAL LABOR Relations Board includes the Board itself, composed of five members (they may sit in panels of three to decide cases), the General Counsel and his staff, and the thirty-one regional offices.

The General Counsel is a very powerful fellow. He has final authority to issue or not to issue a complaint on any charge of an unfair labor practice filed in the regional offices. There is no appeal to any court from his decision not to issue a complaint.

Procedure in Determining If the Union Represents the Majority of the Employees

The authority of the NLRB can be brought to bear in a representation proceeding only by the filing of a petition. Forms for petitions must be signed, sworn to or affirmed under oath, and filed with the regional office in the area where the unit of employees is located. If employees in the unit regularly work in more than one regional area, the petition may be filed with the regional office of any of such regions.

Section 9(c)(1) of the Labor Act provides that when a petition is filed, "the Board shall investigate such petition and if it has reasonable cause to believe that a question of representation affecting commerce exists shall provide for an appropriate hearing upon due notice." If the Board finds from the evidence presented at the hearing that "such a question of representation exists, it shall direct an election by secret ballot and shall certify the results thereof."

If none of the choices on the ballot receives a majority, Section 9(c)(3) provides for a runoff between the choice that received the largest and the choice that received the second largest number of votes in the election. After the election, if a union receives a majority of the votes cast, it is certified by the Board; if no union gets a majority, that result is certified. A union that has been certified is entitled to be recognized by the employer as the exclusive bargaining agent for the employees in the unit. If the employer fails to bargain with the union, he commits an unfair labor practice.

The NLRB has established the policy of not directing an election among employees presently covered by a valid collective-bargaining agreement except in accordance with certain rules. These rules, followed in determining whether or not an existing collective-bargaining contract will bar an election, are called the NLRB contract-bar rules. Not every contract will bar an election. Examples of conditions that would not bar an election are:

The contract is not in writing or is not signed.

The contract has not been ratified by the members of the union, if such is expressly required.

The contract does not contain substantial terms or conditions of employment sufficient to stabilize the bargaining relationship.

The contract can be terminated by either party at any time for any reason.

The contract contains a clearly illegal union-security clause (one requiring an employee to join the union in order to keep his job).

The bargaining unit is not appropriate.

The union that entered the contract with the employer is no longer in existence or is unable or unwilling to represent the employees.

The contract discriminates between employees on racial grounds.

The contracting union is involved in a basic internal conflict, with resulting unstabilizing confusion about the identity of the union.

The employer's operations have changed substantially since the contract was executed.

Under the NLRB rules a valid contract for a fixed period of three years or less will bar an election for the period covered by the contract. A contract for a fixed period of more than three years will bar an election sought by a contracting party during the life of the contract, but will bar an election sought by an outside party for only three years following its effective date. A contract of no fixed period will not act as a bar at all.

If there is no existing contract, a petition can bring about an election if it is filed before the day a contract is signed. If the petition is filed on the same day the contract is signed, the contract bars an election. Once the contract becomes effective as a bar to an election, no petition will be accepted until near the end of the period during which the contract is effective as a bar. Petitions filed not more than ninety days but over sixty days before the end of the contract-bar period will be accepted and can bring about an election. The last sixty days of the contract-bar period is called an "insulated" period. During this time the parties to the existing contract are free to negotiate a new contract or to agree to extend the old one. If they reach agreement in this period, petitions will not be accepted until ninety days before the end of the new contract-bar period. Of course, a petition can be filed after a contract expires.

In addition to the contract-bar rules, the NLRB has established a rule that when a representative has been certified by the Board the certification will ordinarily be binding for at least one year and any petition filed before the end of the certification year will be dismissed. In cases where the certified representative and the employer enter a valid collective-bargaining contract during the year, the contract becomes controlling, and whether a petition for an election can be filed is determined by the Board's contract-bar rules.

Section 9(c)(3) prohibits the holding of an election in any collective-bargaining unit or subdivision thereof in which a valid election has been held during the preceding twelve-month period. A new election may be held, however, in a larger unit, but not in the same unit or subdivision in which the previous election was held. For example, if all of the production and maintenance employees in Company A, including draftsmen in the company engineering office, are included in a collective-bargaining unit, an election among all the employees in the unit, including the draftsmen, would bar another election among all the employees in the unit for twelve months. Similarly, an election among the draftsmen only would bar another election among the draftsmen for twelve months. However, an election among the draftsmen would not bar a later election during the twelve-month period among all the production employees including the draftsmen.

It is the Board's interpretation that Section 9(c)(3) prohibits only the holding of an election during the twelve-month period, but does not prohibit the filing of a petition. Accordingly, the NLRB will accept a petition filed not more than sixty days before the end of the twelve-month period. The election cannot be held, of course, until after the twelve-month period. If an election is held and a representative certified, that certification is binding for one year and a petition for another election in the same unit will be dismissed if it is filed during the one-year period after the certification. If an election is held and no representative is certified, the election bars another election for twelve months. But a petition for another election in the same unit can be filed not more than sixty days before the end of the twelve-month period, and the election can be held after the twelve-month period expires.

Section 9(c)(1) provides that if a question of representation exists, the NLRB must make its determination by means of a secret-ballot election. In a representation election employees are given a choice of one or more bargaining representatives or no representative at all. To be certified as the bargaining representative, an individual or a labor organization must receive a majority of the votes cast.

An election may be held by agreement between the employer and the individual or labor organization claiming to represent the employees. In such an agreement the parties would state the time and place agreed on, the choices to be included on the ballot, and a method to determine who is eligible to vote. They would also authorize the NLRB Regional Director to conduct the election.

34

If the parties are unable to reach an agreement, the Act authorizes the NLRB to order an election after a hearing. The Act also authorizes the Board to delegate to its Regional Directors the determination on matters concerning elections. Under this delegation of authority the Regional Directors can determine the appropriateness of the unit, direct an election, and certify the outcome. Upon the request of an interested party, the Board may review the action of a Regional Director, but such review does not stop the election process unless the Board so orders. The election details are left to the Regional Director. Such matters as who may vote, when the election will be held, and what standards of conduct will be imposed on the parties are decided in accordance with the Board's rules and its decisions.

To be entitled to vote, an employee must have worked in the unit during the eligibility period set by the Board and must be employed in the unit on the date of the election. Generally, the eligibility period is the employer's payroll period just before the date on which the election was directed. This requirement does not apply, however, to employees who are ill, on vacation, or temporarily laid off, or to employees in military service who appear in person at the polls. The NLRB rules take into consideration the fact that employment is typically irregular in certain industries. In such industries eligibility to vote is determined according to formulas designed to permit all employees who have a substantial continuing interest in their employment conditions to vote. Examples of these formulas, which differ from case to case, are:

In one case, employees of a construction company were allowed to vote if they worked for the employer at least sixty-five days during the year before the eligibility date for the election.

In another case, longshoremen who worked at least 700 hours during a specified contract year, and at least twenty hours in each full month between the end of that year and the date on which the election was directed, were allowed to vote.

Radio and television talent employees and musicians in the television film, motion picture, and phonograph-record industries have been held eligible to vote if they worked in the unit two or more days during the year before the date on which the election was directed.

Section 9(c)(3) provides that economic strikers who have been replaced by bona-fide permanent employees may be entitled to vote in an election conducted within twelve months after the commencement of the strike. The permanent replacements are also eligible to vote at the same time. As a general proposition a striker is considered to be an economic striker unless he is found by the NLRB to be on strike over unfair labor practices of the employer. Whether the economic striker is eligible to vote or not is determined on the facts of each case. If he has a new *permanent* job, no.

Ordinarily, elections are held within thirty days after they are directed. Seasonal drops in employment or changes in operations that would prevent a normal work force from being present may cause a different date to be set. It is NLRB practice to postpone an election because of unfair-labor-practice charges, although in certain cases the Board will proceed to the election if the charging party so requests. Also, if a Regional Director dismisses the unfair-labor-practice charges, an election will not be postponed even though an appeal is taken to the General Counsel.

NLRB elections are conducted in accordance with strict standards designed to give the employee-voters an opportunity to freely indicate whether they wish to be represented for purposes of collective bargaining. Election details, such as time, place, and notice of an election, are left largely to the Regional Director, who usually obtains the agreement of the parties on these matters. Any party to an election who believes that the Board's election standards were not met may, within five days after the tally of ballots has been furnished, file objections to the election with the Regional Director under whose supervision the election was held. The Regional Director's rulings on these objections may be appealed to the Board for decision except in the case of elections that are held by consent of the parties, in which case the Regional Director's rulings are final.

An election will be set aside if it was accompanied by conduct that the NLRB considers as having created an atmosphere of confusion or fear of reprisals and thus interfered with the employees' freedom of choice. In any particular case the NLRB does not attempt to determine whether the conduct actually interfered with the employees' expression of free choice, but rather asks whether the conduct tended to do so. If it is reasonable to believe that the conduct would tend to interfere with the free expression of the employees' choice, the election may be set aside. Examples of conduct the Board considers as interfering with employees' free choice are:

Threats of loss of jobs or benefits by an employer or a union to influence the votes or union activities of employees.

Misstatements of important facts in the election campaign by an employer or a union where the other party does not have a fair chance to reply.

An employer's firing employees to encourage or discourage their union activities or a union's causing an employer to take such action.

An employer's or a union's making campaign speeches to assembled groups of employees on company time within the twenty-four-hour period before the election.

The incitement of racial or religious prejudice by inflammatory campaign appeals made by either an employer or a union.

Threats of or the use of physical force or violence against employees by an employer or a union to influence their votes.

The occurrence of extensive violence or trouble or widespread fear of job losses which prevents the holding of a fair election, whether or not caused by an employer or a union.

Procedure in an Unfair-Labor-Practice Case

The procedure in an unfair-labor-practice case is begun by the filing of a charge. A charge may be filed by an employee, an employer, a labor organization, or *any other person*. Like petitions, charge forms must be signed, sworn to or affirmed under oath, and filed with the appropriate regional office—that is, the regional office in the area where the alleged unfair labor practice was committed. Section 10 provides for the issuance of a complaint stating

37

the charges and notifying the charged party of a hearing to be held concerning the charges. Such a complaint will issue only after investigation of the charges by the regional office indicates that an unfair labor practice has in fact occurred.

The hearing is before an NLRB trial examiner and is conducted in accordance with the rules of evidence and procedure that apply in the U.S. district courts. Based on the hearing record, the trial examiner submits his findings and recommendations to the Board. If the Board considers that the person named in the complaint has engaged in or is engaging in the unfair labor practices charged, the Board is authorized to issue an order requiring him to cease and desist from such unfair labor practices and to take appropriate affirmative remedial action—like giving an illegally discharged person back pay.

The NLRB trial examiners are like judges. They are independent of both the Board and the General Counsel. Their appointment and tenure are governed by the Civil Service Commission. When a case is assigned to a trial examiner by the chief trial examiner, the Regional Director and General Counsel step out of the picture. The General Counsel becomes the lawyer for the government and in a sense the lawyer for the person who filed the unfair-labor-practice charge.

With respect to cases assigned to him, the trial examiner has authority to:

Administer oaths and affirmations.

Grant applications for subpoenas.

Rule upon petitions to revoke subpoenas.

Rule upon offers of proof and receive relevant evidence.

Take or cause to be taken depositions whenever the ends of justice would be served thereby.

Regulate the course of the hearing and, if appropriate or necessary, to exclude persons or counsel from the hearing for contemptuous conduct and to strike all related testimony of witnesses refusing to answer any proper question.

Hold conferences for the settlement or simplification of the issues by consent of the parties (but he cannot adjust cases).

Dispose of procedural requests or similar matters, including motions referred to him by the regional director and motions to amend pleadings; also to dismiss complaints or portions thereof, and to order hearings reopened or, upon motion, consolidated prior to issuance of trial-examiner decisions.

Call, examine, and cross-examine witnesses and to introduce into the record documentary or other evidence.

Request the parties at any time during the hearing to state their respective positions concerning any issue in the case or theory in support thereof.

After the trial examiner closes a hearing he writes a decision containing findings of fact, conclusions of law, his evaluation of the credibility of witnesses, and his reasons for his determinations of the issues. He recommends sustaining the complaint or dismissing it. When he issues his decision, the trial examiner steps out of the picture. If the parties do not agree with his recommendations the case goes to the Board, where the trial examiner's decision may be approved, modified, or reversed.

Statute of limitations. Section 10(b) of the Act provides that "no complaint shall issue based upon any unfair labor practice occurring more than six months prior to the filing of the charge with the Board and the service of a copy thereof upon the person against whom such charge is made." The charge must be filed *and* the service made within the six months. Service is made by certified mail, return receipt requested.

If the Regional Director refuses to issue a complaint in a particular case, the person who filed the charge may appeal the decision to the General Counsel in Washington, D.C. Section 3(d) places in the General Counsel "final authority, on behalf of the Board, in respect of the investigation of charges and issuance of complaints." If the General Counsel reverses the Regional Director's decision, he will direct that a complaint be issued. If he approves the decision not to issue a complaint, there is no further appeal.

Powers of the NLRB. To enable the NLRB to perform its duties under the Labor Act, Congress delegated to the Board certain powers that can be used in all cases. These are principally powers having to do with investigations and hearings.

As previously indicated, all charges that are filed with the regional offices are investigated, as are petitions for representation elections. Section 11 establishes the powers of the Board and the regional offices in respect to hearings and investigations. The provisions of Section 11(1) authorize the Board or its agents to:

Examine and copy "any evidence of any person being investigated or proceeded against that relates to any matter under investigation or in question."

Issue subpoenas, on the application of any party to the proceeding, requiring the attendance and testimony of witnesses or the production of any evidence.

Administer oaths and affirmations, examine witnesses, and receive evidence.

Obtain a court order to compel the production of evidence or the giving of testimony.

No person shall be excused from testifying or from producing books, records, correspondence, documents, or other evidence in obedience to the subpoena of the Board on the ground that the testimony or evidence required of him may tend to incriminate him or subject him to a penalty or forfeiture [Section 11(3)]. If he claims his privilege against self-incrimination and is compelled to testify, Section 11(3) protects him from later prosecution on account of anything about which he is compelled to testify. The last provision of Section 11(3) provides that an individual so testifying shall not be exempt from prosecution and punishment for perjury committed in so testifying. Section 12 states that "any person who shall willfully resist, prevent, impede, or interfere with any member of the Board or any of its agents or agencies in the performance of duties pursuant to this Act shall be punished by a fine of not more than $5,000 or by imprisonment for not more than one year, or both."

Except for the foregoing section, which is a limited provision designed solely to keep Board agents from being hampered by interference in their work, the National Labor Relations Act is not a criminal statute. It is entirely remedial. It is intended to prevent and remedy unfair labor practices, not to punish the person responsible for them. The Board is authorized by Section 10(c) not only to issue a cease-and-desist order, but "to take such affirmative action including reinstatement of employees with or without back pay, as will effectuate the policies of this Act."

The object of the Board's order in any case is twofold: to eliminate the unfair labor practice and to undo the effects of the violation as much as possible. In determining what the remedy will be in any given case, the Board has considerable discretion. Ordinarily its order in regard to any particular unfair labor practice will follow a standard form that is designed to remedy that unfair labor practice, but the Board can, and often does, change the standard order to meet the needs of the case. Typical affirmative action of the Board may include orders to an employer who has engaged in unfair labor practices to:

Disestablish an employer-dominated union.

Offer certain named individuals immediate and full reinstatement to their former positions or, if those positions no longer exist, to substantially equivalent positions without prejudice to their seniority and other rights and privileges, and with back pay, including interest.

Upon request, bargain collectively with a certain union as the exclusive representative of the employees in a certain described unit and sign a written agreement if an understanding is reached.

Examples of affirmative action that may be required of a union which has engaged in unfair labor practices include orders to:

Notify the employer and the employees that it has no objection to reinstatement of certain employees, or employment of certain applicants, whose discriminatory discharge, or denial of employment, was caused by the union.

Refund dues or fees illegally collected, plus interest.

Upon request, bargain collectively with a certain employer and sign a written agreement if one is reached.

The Board's order usually includes a direction to the employer or the union, or both, requiring them to post notices notifying the employees that they will cease the unfair labor practices and informing them of any affirmative action being undertaken to remedy the violation. Special care is taken to be sure that these notices are readily understandable by the employees to whom they are addressed.

5

WHY THE RIGHT "APPROPRIATE UNIT" CAN HELP YOU WIN

UNDER THE LABOR Act the union picked by the majority of the employees in an appropriate unit is the exclusive representative of all the employees in that unit "for the purpose of collective bargaining in respect to rates of pay, wages, hours of employment, or other conditions of employment." The Board must "decide in each case whether, in order to assure employees the fullest freedom in exercising the rights guaranteed by this Act, the unit appropriate for the purposes of collective bargaining shall be the employer unit, craft unit, plant unit, or subdivision thereof." The Board has set up guidelines by which to determine the appropriate bargaining unit. The No. 1 rule is that employees with similar interests shall be placed in the same bargaining unit.

The Board decides each case on its own facts. It has broad but not absolute discretion. The Labor Act places a few limitations on that discretion.

Thus Section 9(b)(1) provides that the Board shall not approve as appropriate a unit that includes both professional and nonprofessional employees unless a majority of the professional employees vote to be included in the mixed unit.

Section 9(b)(2) provides that the Board shall not hold a proposed craft unit to be inappropriate simply because a different unit was previously approved by the Board unless a majority of the employees in the proposed craft unit vote against being represented separately.

Section 9(b)(3) prohibits the Board from including plant guards in the same unit with other employees. It also prohibits the

Board from putting its stamp of approval on a labor organization as the representative of a plant guard unit if the labor organization has members who are nonguard employees or if it is "affiliated directly or indirectly" with an organization that has members who are nonguard employees.

Generally, the appropriateness of a bargaining unit is determined on the basis of the common employment interests of the employees involved. Those who have the same or substantially similar interests concerning wages, hours, and working conditions are grouped together in a bargaining unit. In determining whether a proposed unit is appropriate, the following factors are also considered: any history of collective bargaining; the desires of the employees concerned; and the extent to which the employees are organized (Section 9(c)(5) constrains the Board from giving this factor *controlling* weight).

A unit may cover the employees in one plant of an employer, or in two or more plants of the same employer. In some industries where employers are grouped together in voluntary associations, a unit may include employees of two or more employers in any number of locations. It should be noted that a bargaining unit can include only persons who are "employees" within the meaning of the Act. The Act excludes certain types of workers, such as agricultural laborers, independent contractors, and supervisors, from the meaning of "employees." None of these individuals can be included in a bargaining unit established by the Board. In addition, the Board as a matter of policy excludes from bargaining units employees in executive positions and employees who act in a confidential capacity to an employer's labor relations officials.

In most cases where a representation petition has been filed, the parties can reach an agreement with the Regional Director concerning the appropriate unit, and all that remains is the determination whether the majority of employees in the unit want the union to represent them.

Where the parties cannot agree, the Regional Director issues a notice of hearing. A hearing officer hears all the facts the parties present. Then the Regional Director, based on the findings of the hearing officer, makes a determination of the appropriate unit.

The appropriate-unit determination may well decide whether the union will win or lose the election. For example, decisions as to whether an appropriate unit should contain a single plant or store or insurance office or a number of plants or stores or insurance offices may determine the union's chances for ultimate success.

It is always to the employer's advantage to have to deal with only one union. Here are some reasons:

> He has only one set of representatives to deal with.
>
> He has only one contract to negotiate.
>
> The danger of a strike need be faced only once.
>
> He will be spared interunion rivalry (like as not, if Union A wins a 10 percent increase, Union B will strive for a 12 percent increase).
>
> A secure union is more responsible than one in fear of losing its majority.

Where multiunit companies were concerned prior to 1961, the Board tended to favor multistore and multiplant units. Thereafter, however, the Board tended to fragmentize bargaining units by finding that smaller units were appropriate. Thus in *Sav-on Drugs, Inc.* (138 NLRB No. 1032), in 1961, the Board found that a single store was the appropriate unit, rather than all the company's stores in a metropolitan area. In 1963, in *F. W. Woolworth Co.* (144 NLRB No. 307), the Board held that a kitchen staff in a single department store could be considered an appropriate unit in view of their special duties and separate supervision within the store.

There are many other instances of NLRB reversals in the past decade. For example, before 1960:

> The rule was that in the retail-chain field the appropriate bargaining unit should coincide with the employer's administrative division or the geographic area involved. In 1964 the Board found that one restaurant in a city-wide chain was an appropriate unit, calling the former rule "unduly obstructive of effective organization effort." Then the Seventh Circuit Court reversed that ruling, since the restaurant manager had no authority to decide questions affecting the employees in the context of collective bargaining (*Frisch's Big Boy* v. *NLRB*, 356 F.2d 895).

The rule was that in the insurance business the smallest appropriate unit was statewide. The Board in 1961 cut it to a single office (*Quaker State Life Insurance Co.*, 135 NLRB No. 960).

The rule was that only a storewide unit was appropriate in a department store. In 1965 the Board permitted units of selling, nonselling, restaurant, and clerical employees in such stores (*Allied Stores, Inc.*, 170 NLRB No. 79).

Multiple-operation enterprises can organize so that they will not have to deal with several competing unions if they adopt the following procedures:

Hire on an "at large" basis, refraining from stating that prospective employees will work at any one location.

Standardize wages, hours, and working conditions as much as possible.

Make all seniority moves—transfers, promotions, etc.—on an area basis.

Make temporary and permanent interchanges of employees on an area basis as frequently as needed.

Concentrate control of personnel functions in a central location.

Minimize authority and autonomy at local installations to as great a degree as possible.

Obviously, all the foregoing steps must be tempered by sound business judgment.

6

HOW TO KEEP A UNION OUT
OF YOUR PLANT

GET THIS STRAIGHT—there's no sure way. You may treat your employees as if they were your own sons, yet when a union organizer comes around, like as not their reaction will be: "What's the old geezer done for us lately?"

Here's a case that illustrates that if you are nice to your employees you can expect a kick in the teeth!

In this case the company, a bank, was already unionized. The union was not affiliated with any other union; the only members were employees of the bank.

For thirty years the bank had bought stocks and bonds for its employees—both union and nonunion employees—without charging them the fee an outside broker would charge. This hadn't been too much of a burden for the bank in times past. But beginning in 1965 the American people began to go off their rockers about such over-the-counter issues as Greasy Fried Chicken and Last Gasp Nursing Homes. The bank's employees were no exception.

In mid-1968 the bank suddenly realized that employee transactions in securities had jumped 100 percent during the preceding eighteen months. So on July 8, 1968, the bank notified its employees —union and nonunion—that beginning August 1 they would be charged a fee which would be one-half what the bank charged its customers when it performed similar brokerage service for them.

Now if all 3,000 unionized employees were buying and selling stocks the gross amount realized from the fees might be substantial. But the fact was that only ninety out of the 3,000 played around in the market. And if the new fees which were put into effect on August 1 had been in effect throughout 1968, the cost to the ninety employees would have amounted to only $655.21.

The free brokerage service was not mentioned in the contract with the union. The subject was never brought up in negotiations. The contract contained an arbitration clause, but the union did not take the subject of the new fees to arbitration. Instead, it hauled the bank before the Board.

The trial examiner held that the bank had violated the Act by failing to bargain with the union before unilaterally imposing the fees. *Imposing*, that's the word the trial examiner used! The bank was ordered to reimburse the employees for fees it had collected (*Seattle First National Bank*, 77 LRRM 2634).

Gratitude, huh? See what you're up against?

But you can try!

How to win. What you—and particularly your supervisors— have to do is to treat your employees so that their instinctive reaction when an organizer asks them to sign authorization cards will be to say: "What do we need a union for? We don't want a union. Why should we pay dues to some outsider?"

This rebuff to the union is likely to occur if the following conditions of employment exist in your plant:

Wages and fringe benefits are as good or better than those in effect at unionized plants in the same or related businesses in the area.

Seniority is observed in such matters as promotions, job assignments, and vacation and shift preferences unless it is quite obvious to everyone that in a particular instance it should not be observed.

Discipline is administered impartially and consistently.

Plant rules are explained clearly and concisely in writing.

Privileges are not granted to some and withheld from others.

A formal grievance procedure is maintained in good faith so that an employee can obtain a hearing before higher authority if he feels he has been treated unjustly by a supervisor.

The last condition is the most important of all. The grievance procedure must be in writing and available to everyone. (The terms can be contained in the booklet given to each employee explaining the plant rules and fringe benefits.)

The grievance procedure should provide for a hearing before the employee's supervisor's supervisor. If the decision of the latter does not satisfy the employee, he should be able to present his case to someone even higher in the chain of command. If the decision of this person does not satisfy the employee in *discharge cases only* he should be able to present his case to an impartial third party whose decision should be final and binding on both the employee and the company.

In this procedure the employee should be allowed to have someone represent him—either a fellow employee or an outsider. If a discharge goes to arbitration, the company should pay the arbitrator's fee, at the same time assuring the arbitrator that it wants him to hear the case just as if a union were representing the employee and paying one-half the arbitrator's fee.

Here is an example of what is meant. It is a quotation from a decision by one of the country's foremost arbitrators:

The grievant, on the morning of July 28, 1967, at approximately 3:00 A.M. o'clock, drove his motorcycle with a passenger on board into the company's parking lot and then proceeded through a door and into the plant proper . . . It is alleged that the grievant was intoxicated, or under the influence of alcoholic beverage . . . He drove past stacks of glass and through areas where fork-lift trucks were being operated, and other employees were at work. He then turned about and retraced his path out of the plant. The fact that no one was injured by the grievant's immature and reckless adventure is not of a mitigating significance; it in no way detracts from the seriousness of the grievant's misconduct . . . A plant is not the proper arena for display of motorcycle prowess, horseplay, or other forms of daredevil inclinations . . .

The instant arbitration is unique. There are 750 hourly employees of the company at its Crestline Works. The employees are not members of any employee organization or association. However, there is in effect an "Employees Handbook" prepared and distributed by the company and designed to set forth the terms and conditions of employment which have been recognized by management as constituting employee benefits . . .

The proceeding is unusual in that it constitutes an appeal from a decision of management to discharge the aggrieved employee for alleged misconduct and violation of the plant rules set forth in the Handbook. The arbitrator was selected in accordance with the procedure outlined in the Handbook for the resolution of employee grievances. At the very outset it was made clear to the arbitrator that his conduct of the hearing and the evaluation of the evidence were to adhere to established principles governing the arbitration of employee disputes . . . Both management and the aggrieved employee were represented during the arbitration proceeding by management personnel. The case on behalf of the aggrieved employee was presented and developed by none other than the Manager of Industrial Relations. The position of the company was presented and developed by the Plant Manager. The arbitration was extensive in scope and included extensive evidentiary background . . . The arbitrator was impressed by the extraordinary and able presentation by the Manager of Industrial Relations; he demonstrated forthrightness, courage and absence of any extraneous fears in his defense of the grievant's right. It was quite apparent that there was no element of compromise or inhibition in the challenge advanced on behalf of the aggrieved employee as regard the contentions that the discharge penalty was unsupported by evidence or just cause and that the penalty was unjustly harsh and severe . . .

The matter was appealed to arbitration in accordance with the procedure outlined in the Employees Handbook, to wit:

"ITEM 33: ARBITRATION PROCEDURE

"It is the desire of Management that the employees of this Plant be secure in their employment and that they have no fear that their employment will be terminated without good and sufficient reason. We are, therefore, establishing the following arbitration procedure which we are confident will give our employees the security they desire and which we wish them to have.

"Eligibility—

"This procedure is available to any employee who is on the hourly seniority list and has at least two years' seniority at the time of his termination.

"Procedure—

"Step 1. An eligible employee who wishes to have his discharge submitted to arbitration shall submit his request in writing to the Plant Manager within forty-eight hours of the time he receives his payoff slip.

"Step 2. The Plant Manager shall request the American Arbitration Association, Cleveland, Ohio, for a list of three arbitrators, all of whom reside within a reasonable distance of Crestline. The list, together with a biographical sketch of each of the arbitrators, shall be given to the Grievant. . . .

"The Grievant, if he so desires, can request that a member of Management shall help prepare his presentation.

"Arbitrator's Authority—

"The issue in each case shall be whether the Grievant was discharged for just cause. In making his determination the arbitrator shall be governed by the plant's disciplinary rules and procedures. Should the arbitrator sustain the grievance, he may order reinstatement, including back pay should he find the circumstances warrant it . . .

"The cost of the arbitration proceeding shall be paid for by the Company . . ."

Although the grievant's misconduct constituted just cause for severe disciplinary treatment, in light of the mitigating circumstances including the grievant's satisfactory work record and relatively long tenure of service, the penalty of discharge will be vacated and the grievant directed to be reinstated, without back pay [*Pittsburgh Plate Glass Company*, 39 Labor Arbitration Reports 370, Harry J. Dworkin, Cleveland, Arbitrator].

A procedure like the above is very effective in keeping a union out of your plant. But it requires that your supervisors be exemplary individuals. They must be able to take a reversal of a discharge without directing animosity toward the reinstated employee.

A common reaction to the above suggestion is: "My door is always open. If anyone gets a raw deal from a supervisor he can come to me and I'll straighten out the supervisor."

Alas, employees don't enter the "open door." Some are scared. Some are inarticulate. And there are among supervisors some s.o.b.s who can be very subtle about "getting" anyone who passes through the open door.

7

HOW TO WIN WHEN A UNION ORGANIZER
MAKES YOUR PLANT HIS TARGET

DON'T PANIC AND do something which may make it possible for the NLRB to order you to bargain with a union despite the fact that no election has been held to determine whether your employees want to be represented by this union, that union, or no union. If the organizer holds out a bunch of cards and says they have been signed by a majority of your employees to authorize the union to represent them in bargaining with you concerning wages, hours, and other terms and conditions of employment, *do not touch the cards.* Push them back at him and tell him to petition the NLRB to hold an election.

The classic case of a man panicking is the Monahan case (*Monahan Ford,* 157 NLRB No. 88).

Monahan had a Ford agency, where he employed nineteen mechanics. A union organizer named Diamond set out to organize these people. He held a meeting at the home of one of the mechanics and obtained signatures of fifteen of them on cards authorizing the union to represent them.

Monahan caught wind of this and questioned one of the mechanics. The Board held that Monahan's purpose was to chill the mechanics' effort to bargain through a representative of their own choosing. So it was an unfair labor practice—interference with the right of self-organization.

Next, Monahan's service manager approached a group of the mechanics and said that he knew what they were up to and that they should think twice before they did it. Another unfair labor practice—a veiled threat of reprisal.

Next, Monahan laid off Gorman, at whose home the meeting had been held, ostensibly for lack of work. But the facts indicated that if the union hadn't been in the picture Gorman would not have been laid off. Another unfair labor practice.

Next, Diamond showed up at Monahan's office accompanied by twelve of the mechanics and demanded that Monahan recognize the union as bargaining agent for "*all* your employees." When a union organizer demands that a company bargain, he must "clearly define the unit for which recognition is sought." Monahan had a couple of clerical workers. But a reasonable man would have known that Diamond meant the mechanics when he said "all your employees." So Monahan committed another unfair labor practice—refusal to bargain when he knew that a majority of the nineteen mechanics (twelve) wanted the union as their bargaining agent.

There doesn't have to be an election. There don't have to be signed authorization cards. When, as here, action by the majority of an appropriate bargaining unit makes it clear that they want a certain union to represent them, the duty to bargain arises.

The mechanics went out on strike, whereupon Monahan sent each striker a telegram threatening that failure to report for work the next day would mean that the company would seek a replacement for him.

A company has the right to replace economic strikers with newly hired employees. But this strike was not an economic strike; it was to protest "what the *employees* regarded as the company's unlawful refusal to bargain," in the words of the Trial Examiner. As such, it was an activity protected by the Labor Act. Monahan's telegram implied a threat for engaging in this protected activity— another unfair labor practice.

After a few days the union threw in the sponge. On behalf of the mechanics, it made an unconditional offer to return to work. Monahan refused to reinstate some of the strikers for whom he had hired replacements. But an employer must let replacements go and reinstate "unfair-labor-practice strikers" (as distinguished from "economic strikers," who are striking for higher wages or better working conditions), so this was yet another unfair labor practice.

54

Monahan, poor fellow, was not only ordered to give the mechanics the back pay they had lost but also to sit down and bargain with the union.

Chances are that if Monahan's mechanics had not struck and Diamond had proffered him the cards, he would have taken them and ascertained that indeed the cards did contain signatures of a majority of the nineteen mechanics, and he would have been ordered to bargain with the union even though, if he had not taken them, the mechanics in the privacy of the voting booth might have voted "no union." Or he would have told the union to request the NLRB to set an election and then have made a speech promising the mechanics benefits if they voted against the union or threatening them with reprisals if they voted for the union. In either case he would be committing an unfair labor practice and would probably be ordered to bargain with the union even if the vote was 19 to 0 against the union.

Steps to Take. When you sense that a union organizer is sniffing around, the first thing to do is to determine whether your business affects interstate commerce (see page 23). In ninety-nine cases out of a hundred it does. The next thing to do is to determine whether the NLRB will handle your case, that is, whether the dollar volume of your business is sufficient to cause it to fall within the Board's jurisdictional standards (see pages 24-25). If the answer to this question is negative, you'd better start worrying about your state labor relations law. See a labor relations lawyer.

The next thing to do is to post a statement of your position on all bulletin boards. This statement must not offer the employees benefits if they turn their backs on the union or threaten them with reprisals if they embrace it. Such a statement is difficult to draft because the NLRB and the courts read into employer statements threats that the employer never intended.

However, the Sixth Circuit Court refused to enforce a Board order condemning the following bulletin notice as "veiled threats":

As you know, unions are again campaigning to organize some of our employees. Some of you are again asking questions regarding this campaign. Because of your questions, we are stating the Company's position on this matter as clearly as possible.

(1) This matter is, of course, one of concern to the Company. It is also a matter of serious concern to you. Our sincere belief is that if a union were to represent you in our plant, it would not work to your benefit.

(2) We sincerely believe that the introduction of a union into our plant is not necessary or beneficial to your welfare and growth with this Company. We, therefore, propose to use every proper means to prevent a union from becoming established here.

(3) We would like to make it clear that it is not necessary for anyone to belong to any union in order to work in this plant.

(4) Those who might join or belong to a union will not receive any advantages over those who do not join or belong to a union.

(5) If anyone causes you any trouble at your work or puts you under any kind of pressure to join a union, you should let the Company know, and we will undertake to see that this is stopped.

(6) No person will be allowed to carry on union organization activities on the job. Anyone who does so and who thereby neglects his work or interferes with the work of others will be subject to discharge.

You should be aware that the above statements are factual and that any information you may receive which is in conflict to this is not true. Please feel free to continue to discuss any questions or problems that you may have concerning these matters with either Mr. Paul Gordon or any supervisory employee [*Suprenant Manufacturing Co.* v. *NLRB*, 341 F.2d 756].

You may bar the organizer from your property. The Supreme Court has held that you may call the cops and have a union organizer who is passing out literature in your parking lot ejected unless the distances between the plant and the employees' homes place the employees beyond the reach of reasonable union efforts to communicate with them (*NLRB* v. *Babcock & Wilcox Co.*, 351 U.S. 105). Most of the employees at the Babcock & Wilcox plant lived in a small town nearby, so the company had the right to eject the organizer.

On the other hand, if your plant is located in a large city and outside union organizers would not be able to distribute literature (except by standing at a busy intersection), you must permit them to distribute the literature while standing on your property; you cannot eject them without violating the Act (*Solo Cup Co.,* 172 NLRB No. 110).

The Board has also held that where a vendor's employees serviced vending machines in various plants and the company had a rule that its employees who performed services on the premises of its customers were not to solicit for a union and an employee did so solicit, the customer had the right to have that employee removed from the premises. The customer did so, and moreover the vendor company fired the employee.

The Board held that the vendor's rule was valid. It referred to the rule permitting a retail store to forbid union solicitation by employees during nonworking hours in parts of the store open to the public, citing *Marshall Field & Co.* (98 NLRB No. 88). It also held that the customer did not violate the rule when he had the vendor's employee removed from the premises (*Sylvania Electric Products,* 174 NLRB No. 159).

Rules concerning employee solicitation for a union and distribution of union literature. Don't wait until a union organizer appears; post these rules NOW: "Soliciting for any cause whatsoever during working hours is strictly forbidden. Working time is for work"; and "Distribution of literature within the working areas of the plant is forbidden at all times."

This means no soliciting during working hours for the Red Cross, flowers for a sick fellow-employee, etc. The rule must be strictly enforced; if it is not, and you try to enforce it where soliciting for a union is concerned, you can be charged with illegal discrimination.

You cannot forbid your employees to solicit for a union on company property during nonworking time. If you run a retail store, however, you can forbid solicitation during nonworking hours in public areas of the store.

You cannot ban distribution of literature by employees on the parking lot and other places outside the working area, but you can impose a rule against littering the place.

The NLRB has held that a company rule which prohibits employees from entering or returning to the plant during their non-working time to solicit union support in nonworking areas is invalid unless the company can show that such a rule is necessary in order to maintain production discipline, or for the safety of the plant. The Board overruled a decision by a trial examiner that the rule was valid because the work relationship with the plant did not exist after the employees' shift was finished and thus the employer could deny access to the plant to the employees as if they were strangers.

In the above case, the employees worked on the day shift and returned to the plant at 11 P.M., when the graveyard shift was going on duty and the night shift was leaving. Access from the street was through a gate which led immediately into the employees' locker room.

The company's argument that the rule was necessary for plant security and safety was rejected because, although it was able to prove thefts and dangerous gas leakages, it could not show that the incidents involved the off-duty employees (*Diamond Shamrock Co.*, 181 NLRB No. 43).

Prohibiting the wearing of buttons. Employees have the right to wear buttons in the plant that plug the union (*Republic Aviation Corp.* v. *NLRB*, 324 U.S. 793), but not a button bearing a legend like "Don't Be a Scab. Join the Union." For the employee's right to self-organization must give way to the employer's paramount right to maintain discipline in the plant (*Caterpillar Tractor Co.* v. *NLRB* 230 F.2d 357).

What if the employees come in contact with the public?

A trial examiner has held that a company did not violate the Labor Act when it suspended and discharged twenty drivers, whose job was to deliver small packages to members of the public, for violating a rule which, in effect, prohibited the drivers from wearing on their uniforms a white button two and one-half inches in diameter with a legend in red reading "Vote Jack Ryan Local 294" (*United Parcel Service, Inc.*, Case 3-CA-4118 [1970]).

The trial examiner held that since Ryan was running for a

union office, the wearing of a Ryan button was a protected activity under Section 7 of the Act, for employees have as much interest in who represents them in their affairs with the employer as they have in fixing the terms of their collective-bargaining agreement. He noted that it is established law that employees have the right while at work to wear a union button or other insignia related to concerted activities except under certain special circumstances.

On the other hand, the trial examiner said, the company had the right to prohibit the drivers from wearing the Ryan button while in the company uniform on their delivery routes. Weighing the conflicting rights, he decided that the balance favored the company. In giving up the right to wear the button, the employees were not giving up much, as the chances were slim they would run into other members of Local 294 while on their route. The button's message was aimed only at such members.

So the trial examiner concluded that the company order prohibiting the wearing of the Ryan button while away from the plant did not violate the Act.

Freedom of speech, NLRB style. Once the NLRB orders a representation election, the election campaign period begins. The first thing the company must do is to file with the Board a list of the names and addresses of the employees in the bargaining unit. This is called the *Excelsior Underwear* rule. It was adopted in 1966.

Here is the gist of the rule: Within seven days after the NLRB Regional Director has approved a consent-election agreement or the Board has directed an election, the employer must file with the Regional Director an election eligibility list containing the names and addresses of all the eligible voters. The Regional Director must make this information available to the union. Failure to comply with the requirement will be grounds for setting aside the election if an objection is filed.

If the payroll period for eligibility purposes falls after the election order or consent-election agreement, the eligibility list must be filed within seven days after the close of the determinative payroll period for eligibility purposes. The list must be *received* by the Regional Director within the period required (*Excelsior Underwear, Inc.*, 156 NLRB No. 111).

Among the many reasons the Board gave for issuing the new rule was the alleged fact that after twenty months of organizational efforts directed against *May Department Stores, Inc.* (136 NLRB No. 797), the union had names and addresses of only 1,250 out of approximately 3,000 eligible voters. The Board said that without a list of employee names and addresses, a labor organization has no method by which it can be certain of reaching all the employees with its argument in favor of representation. It added that the rule was necessary to ensure an informed electorate.

The moment the Board orders an election, the company, all the way down to the lowest-ranking supervisor, must be very careful what it says or the Board may rule that it has been interfering with the employees' Section 7 rights to assist unions, act in concert, etc. (see page 68) or that the "laboratory conditions" it requires for an election have been tainted. In such an event, the Board will then set aside an election the company has won and order a new election.

Section 8(c) of the Labor Act states that expression of any views by management shall *not* constitute evidence of an unfair labor practice if such expression contains no threat of reprisal or promise of benefit. The First Amendment is supposed to protect freedom of speech during an election campaign. But the NLRB holds that even if an employer's statement contains no *express* threats, it may be coercive simply because of the circumstances of the employer-employee relationship. The Board considers *the actual words used as irrelevant;* what counts is what the speaker intended and how the listener understood him.

Former U.S. Solicitor General Archibald Cox, a Board apologist, has put it this way: "Words which may only antagonize a hard-bitten Detroit truck driver may seriously intimidate a rural textile hand in a company village where the mill owner dominates every aspect of life."

This is a lot of applesauce. In most of the cases that reach the Board involving picket-line violence it's the rural textile hands who rock cars, break windshields, punch nonstrikers, and throw tacks in the driveway. There are few employees today who are "intimidated" by the boss's words.

Nevertheless, in his last opinion before leaving the bench, Chief Justice Earl Warren of the Supreme Court bought this highly questionable theory. He said in *NLRB* v. *Gissel Packing Co.* (395 U.S. 575) that the court agreed with the lower court that "conveyance of the employer's belief *even though sincere* that unionization will or may result in the closing of the plant is not a statement of fact unless, which is most improbable, the eventuality of closing is capable of proof."

Don't ever make a speech to assembled employees unless it has been approved in advance by a labor relations lawyer to whom you have revealed *all* that you and your supervisors have done theretofore in fighting unionism.

Here are some things that must not be said, some things you may consider saying, and some things you ought to say:

AVOID SAYING:

- Bargaining will start from scratch.
- A strike will be inevitable.
- The union intends to impose noncompetitive conditions on you as the employer.
- The plant may close if the union wins the election.
- If the union wins and a strike occurs you will contract out production work.
- If the union causes a strike you will permanently replace strikers.
- The blacks will come in here.
- You can promise the employees a year-round job and they won't have to pay dues to get it.
- If the employees choose the union, both they and the company will be hurt economically.
- Anything you can't easily substantiate as being true.
- You won't bargain until a circuit court orders you to do so.

- The employees have everything to gain and nothing to lose by rejecting the union.
- If the union gets in here it would do the employees serious harm.
- NLRB orders are easily circumvented.

CONSIDER SAYING:

- Present benefits may not necessarily continue under a union contract.
- The union has quite a strike record.
- If the union makes unreasonable demands leading to a strike you will exercise your right to permanently replace the strikers, which means they will lose their jobs at least until their replacements quit.
- Unions can't create jobs.
- The employees have benefits that employees at unionized plants don't have.

BE SURE TO SAY:

- A majority of those who vote, not a majority of all employees in the unit, will decide the election.
- The election will be secret; no one will know how anyone voted.
- Prior signing of a union authorization card does not require voting for the union.
- No union can obtain more than you as an employer are *able* to give.
- Employees can no longer come to you confidentially with their troubles in the plant.
- The following statements made by the organizer are false (quote, then refute).

NOTE

There are signs that with the advent of Nixon appointees on the Board, employers may be given more leeway. In a 1971 case NLRB chairman Edward B. Miller, a Nixon appointee in 1970, dissenting from a majority opinion by members Fanning and Jenkins, has:

Called attention to the existence of Section 8(c).

Expressed the opinion that an employer *may* tell employees that he does not intend to agree to any demands he thinks are not in their best interests, or which he opposes as a matter of principle, such as the union shop.

Expressed the opinion that an employer may tell employees that the union might call a strike if its demands are not met, and that the company would replace those employees who went on strike.

Expressed the opinion that no violation of the Labor Act was committed by an employer who, before the union appeared on the scene, was exploring the possibility of expanding the employees' insurance coverage and had contracted two insurance brokers for this purpose, and after the election petition has been filed, informed the employees of this fact and after the union lost the election put the increased insurance benefits into effect (*Tommy's Spanish Foods, Inc.*, 187 NLRB No. 31).

Activities an employer must avoid during an election campaign:

Making a speech on company time and property of even the most innocuous type to mass assemblies of employees within the twenty-four hours before the election. This is known as the *Peerless Plywood* rule, from the name of the case in which it was first enunciated. Violate this rule and the election will be set aside whichever party wins.

Interviewing employees individually or in small groups away from their work stations in a private office or other place of management authority.

Using reproductions of the official ballot as campaign propaganda.

Interrogating employees.

Running a want ad for new employees just before the election.

Discussing the election with employees called to the supervisor's desk.

Discharging or otherwise disciplining employees if you know they are union activists. Even though you firmly believe that a union activist ought to be disciplined, don't do it unless he is caught red-handed doing some atrocious thing. Trial examiners are adept at finding that your real motivation for imposing the discipline was your opposition to the employee's union activity, not the fact that he was caught damaging company property or whatever. Indeed in a small plant they will find that you knew he was a union activist even though in fact you didn't know.

Placing employees under surveillance or giving the impression to employees that you are doing so.

Urging the formation of a committee so that you can deal directly with it rather than with "some outsider"; in other words, don't advocate the formation of a "company union."

Eliminating benefits.

Granting benefits unless you can thereafter prove that you would have granted the benefits even though the union was not in the picture. A tough thing to prove.

Using Madison Avenue tactics to get employees to vote, unless it is made crystal clear that you want the employees to vote in any case, not just for "no union."

As to pre-election parties given by the employer, the Board has said in a case where an election was won by the company:

This would not justify setting aside the election, for the Board has held that the furnishing of free food and drink is a permissible electioneering activity, and, assuming that there could be anything wrong with live entertainment, there is no evidence of any such entertainment, unless it be jitterbugging by the employees themselves. The Board has also refused to constitute itself a temperance society, and thus even the furnishing of alcoholic beverages—in this case, the beer—has been held to be permissible electioneering, certainly so long as such beverages have been consumed in moderation [*Peachtree City Warehouse, Inc.*, 158 NLRB No. 97].

But the employer must beware of campaigning at such a party. For example, he must not show antiunion movies like *And Women Must Weep* or *A Question of Law and Order*. He must avoid being victimized by his friends. If the mayor of the town or the pastor of the local church threatens that the sky will fall or the plant will close if the union wins the election, the employer should repudiate him. Above all, he must not make any appeals to racial prejudice, and he must not misrepresent facts.

Many of the things mentioned above may be done by *unions* to influence voters in ways condemned by NLRB as not in keeping with the "laboratory conditions" it seeks when holding an election. Probably the last item is the most important. The NLRB will set aside an election won by the union if it is established that the union misrepresented facts that may reasonably be expected to have had a significant impact on the election. It's a good idea for an employer to keep a file of all letters, flyers, etc., used by the union during the campaign.

8

HOW THE EMPLOYEES' REPRESENTATIVE
IS CHOSEN NORMALLY

SECTION 9(c)(1) OF THE Labor Act provides that a secret-ballot election shall be conducted by the NLRB whenever the question arises as to whether a union or no union shall represent employees. (Unfortunately, the Board has developed another method of choosing employee representatives without the safeguard of a secret-ballot election. See page 101.)

If you are sure your employees don't want a union, the best thing to do is to agree that an election may be held. The agreement will cover such matters as the place and time of the election and a method of determining which employees are eligible to vote. The NLRB Regional Director is authorized to conduct the election.

If you are not sure that your employees will vote "no union," the best thing to do is to let the union that claims to represent them carry the ball by petitioning for an election. The NLRB is authorized to order an election after a hearing. It also is authorized to delegate this function to the Regional Director. The Regional Director can determine the appropriate unit, order that the election be held, and certify the result. To be certified as the bargaining representative of the employees in an appropriate unit, the union must receive a majority of the votes cast. If there's a tie, the union loses. Elections are usually held within thirty days after they are directed.

The Board's regulations govern such matters as who may vote, when the election will be held, and how the parties must conduct themselves.

To be able to vote, an employee must be employed in the unit on the date of the election. He must also have worked in the unit for a period of time known as the eligibility period. Usually the eligibility period is the employer's payroll period ending before the election date.

In any election conducted within twelve months after the beginning of an economic strike, the strikers are allowed to vote even if they have been permanently replaced. The permanent replacements may also be eligible to vote in the same election. The general rule is that a striker is an economic striker seeking better wages or benefits unless the NLRB finds that he is on strike protesting an unfair labor practice of the employer.

The NLRB endeavors to conduct elections under very strict standards. But you should be alert to see that security of the ballot box is not violated.

In one case, for example, a company located in Vermont held a split-session election at its plant in Middlebury. After the first session the ballot box was sealed and taped, and signatures were affixed. But in putting the cardboard ballot box together, the Board agent in charge of the election used masking tape (which can be easily removed without leaving a trace) instead of gummed paper (which always leaves a mark). Moreover, signatures on the masking tape were not continued onto the cardboard ballot box to ensure that the tape could not be easily removed and replaced without leaving indications of tampering. The slot through which ballots were dropped was also sealed with masking tape instead of gummed paper.

After the sealing procedures had been completed, the Board agent stored the ballot box in the rear of his station wagon. Beside it he placed his leather briefcase containing blank ballots. Then he locked the station wagon, and he and the company and union observers went into a diner for a cup of coffee. The ballot box and blank ballots remained in the locked station wagon, parked fifty feet from the diner, for the thirty minutes during which the Board agent and the observers were in the diner.

After the second session the ballot box was again sealed and signatures affixed in the same manner as before. The agent took his leave of the observers and drove to the Middlebury Inn, where he was staying. He parked in front of the inn and, covering the ballot box with a sweater, again placed the box in the rear of the station wagon, which he locked. Next he locked the briefcase con-· taining the blank ballots in his room. He then had lunch and strolled around the town. The station wagon, the ballot box, and the blank ballots remained untended for three hours.

When the ballot box was opened for a tabulation of the votes, the company's suspicions were aroused by the appearance of many ballots in neatly creased stacks. Also, since many employees had voluntarily approached the company and assured it that the outcome of the election would be a repetition of the prior year's election, in which another union had contended for representation rights, the shift in sentiment caused the company to question the security of the ballot box. For this time the vote was 73 to 51 in favor of the union, whereas in the previous year's election 92 employees had voted "no union" as against only 29 who embraced the union.

The company thereafter asserted that the failure of the Board agent to adhere to appropriate safeguards in the sealing and custody of the ballot box and in the security of the blank ballots required that the election be set aside, due to the existence of a "possibility of irregularity."

The Regional Director found that the Board agent did maintain desirable election standards. The Board adopted his findings and certified the union as representative of the employees.

The circuit court approved an NLRB rule that the Board may certify election results despite procedural deficiencies in the conduct of the election that make it impossible for the Board to state with certainty that no tampering with the ballot box has occurred. (*Polymers, Inc.* v. *NLRB*, 71 LRRM 3107).

How to win. If you believe that the Board's election standards were not met you may, within five days after the tally of ballots has been furnished, file objections to the election with the Regional Director under whose supervision the election was held. If he rules against you, an exception to his ruling may be filed with the Board for decision. This is one case where if you consented to the election, you are out of luck, for the Regional Director's ruling on objections is final.

The Section 7 Rights of Employees

The principal rights of employees specifically guaranteed to them are set out in Section 7 of the Labor Act, which reads as follows:

"Employees shall have the right to self-organization, to form, join, or assist labor organizations, to bargain collectively through representatives of their own choosing, and to engage in other concerted activities for the purpose of collective bargaining or other mutual aid or protection, and shall also have the right to refrain from any or all of such activities except to the extent that such right may be affected by an agreement requiring membership in a labor organization as a condition of employment as authorized in section 8(a)(3)."

The reference to Section 8(a)(3) means that an employee has the right *not* to join a union unless under certain conditions the union and the employer have made an agreement that employees must join the union in order to keep their jobs.

This kind of an agreement is called a union security agreement or a union-shop agreement, and since it imposes union membership on an employee whether he wills it or not, it is fenced around with all kinds of conditions and protections favoring the employee. See next chapter, "Union Security Agreements."

Here are some examples of employees' rights protected by Section 7:

Forming or attempting to form a union among the employees of a company.

Joining a union whether the union is recognized by the employer or not.

Assisting a union to organize an employer.

Going out on strike to secure better working conditions.

Refraining from activity in behalf of a union.

9

UNION SECURITY AGREEMENTS

A UNION SECURITY agreement is one which enables a union to get paid for representing employees. For a union security agreement to be valid, it must meet all the following requirements:

The union must not be assisted or controlled by the employer [Section 8(a)(2)].

The union must be the majority representative of the employees in the appropriate collective-bargaining unit covered by such agreement when made.

The union's authority to make such an agreement must not have been revoked within the previous twelve months by the employees in a Board election.

The agreement must provide for at least a thirty-day grace period after hire during which he need not pay the union any money (seven days in the building and construction industry).

There are four principal types of union security agreements:

A closed-shop agreement, which requires that a person be a member of the union before he may be hired. Closed-shop agreements are illegal.

A union-shop agreement, which requires an employee to become a union member on or after the thirtieth day after he is hired or after the agreement is signed. The employee not only must join the union and pay the initiation fee, but he must keep his dues paid or the union can demand that the employer fire him.

A maintenance-of-membership agreement, which requires an employee who is a union member when the agreement is signed to remain a member and keep his dues paid if he is to retain his job.

An agency-shop agreement, which, although it doesn't require an employee to join the union, does require him to pay the union the equivalent of union dues in order to keep his job.

These union security agreements may be declared illegal by state laws (about nineteen states have adopted such laws). Some state laws allow an agency-shop agreement but forbid a union-shop agreement. These laws are called "right to work" laws.

Employers must be on their guard when one of these agreements is part of the labor contract because a union can demand that an employer fire an employee only for either of two reasons: failure to join the union thirty days after he is hired or after the labor contract becomes effective, whichever is later, or failure to pay his dues. If an employer fires an employee on the demand of a union for any other reason he will be found guilty of an unfair labor practice, i.e., illegally encouraging union membership.

It is an unfair labor practice for a union to attempt to cause a company to discharge an employee pursuant to the usual union-shop clause because the employee, already a union member in good standing, refuses to pay an "admission fee" called for by the union's bylaws to exact a larger share of financial support from a member when promoted to a higher-paid job classification. A union had endeavored to justify this conduct by labeling the required payment as an initiation fee uniformly required as a condition of acquiring or retaining membership. The NLRB trial examiner held that the phrase "initiation fees" as used in the statute must be construed as meaning a payment "uniformly required for the purpose of admission into membership of a labor organization" (*Aluminum Workers Trade Council,* Case No. 19-CB-1423 [1970]).

If an employee tells his supervisor that he had not been notified of his obligation to pay nominal dues while on layoff and the supervisor takes no action to investigate the truth of the employee's claim, discharge by the company at the request of the union for nonpayment of dues is a violation of the Labor Act.

In this case the union failed to notify the employee in unambiguous language that while on layoff he was required to purchase "unemployment stamps" at a cost of 50 cents a month in lieu of paying dues and that he would become delinquent after ninety days. The particular employee was on layoff for six months.

After the employee was recalled, he told his supervisor about the union's failure to notify him about the stamps. The supervisor made no efforts to inquire of the union whether this was true. Instead, when the request came through for the employee's discharge, the company complied.

The trial examiner ruled that the union and the company were at fault and ordered both to reinstate the employee in good standing. The union has a duty to inform even a veteran employee of the action he must take to protect his job, and if the company has even an inkling that this duty has not been fulfilled, it will be hooked if it fires the employee (*Conductron Corporation*, Case 14-CA-5090 [1970]).

When a union wins a union security clause in a contract, it usually also tries to get the employer to agree to check off the dues from the employee's wages. Employers cannot agree to do this without a written authorization from the employee. Quite obviously, if the company has control of the payment of an employee's dues and the union comes around and asks that the employee be discharged, the reason must be other than the failure to tender the periodic dues.

Where there is no checkoff system in effect, the employer must do some investigating when the union demands that an employee be fired for nonpayment of dues. It is his duty to determine the truth of the matter.

The three cases outlined below bear on the union-security problem.

In the first case, the Board held three to two that a company legally discharged a female clerk in a Seattle retail store at the request of the union because she refused to pay her dues.

The company and the union had entered into an oral contract. One of its "clauses" required employees to belong to the union as a condition of keeping their jobs. The company and the union negotiators had agreed on a welfare clause, a wage increase, and a

71

contract effective date. They failed to reach agreement, they testified, on hours of employment but decided to defer that item and
consider that they had a "deal." Neither asked the other to commit
the agreement to writing.

The twelve employees ratified the agreement by a ten-to-two
vote after the terms, including the union-shop provision, had been
explained to them.

Pat Davis joined the union and paid three months' dues. But she
was distressed by the failure to agree on the hours of work, and
when no agreement had been reached in the fourth month she
refused to pay any more dues. The union negotiator called the
company negotiator. Before you could say Jack Robinson, Pat was
a candidate for unemployment compensation.

Pat charged both the company and the union with unfair labor
practices.

Three Board members voted to dismiss the complaint. They
argued that since the Act does not require a collective-bargaining
agreement to be reduced to writing unless requested by either
party and that since the union-shop provision was part and parcel
of the collective-bargaining agreement, it was not required to be
in writing.

"The logic is flawless," said the two dissenting members, "but
what about policy?" Because of the drastic consequences (job
loss) visited upon employees who fail to comply with a union
security clause, they thought the Board should have ruled that a
union security clause must be in writing if it is to be used to defend
a discharge at the request of a union (*Pacific Iron and Metal Co.*,
175 NLRB No. 114).

Under a union security agreement, a new employee must have
a thirty-day grace period before being obliged to sign with the
union. If the company's hiring procedure does not make this clear,
both the company and the union will be in the soup. In this case,
the company and union were parties to a lawful thirty-day union-
shop contract. When an employee was hired, he was asked by a
company clerk if he was a member of the union. If the new employee said no, the clerk would tell him that he had to join the

union and would hand him an application for union membership and a dues-deduction authorization form entitled "Employee's Voluntary Declaration." The employee was told that the monthly dues were four dollars and that the company would deduct that amount from his paycheck and pay it to the union. Employees invariably signed these forms on being hired and had their dues checked off effective as of the date of hiring. (One of the clerks in the personnel office testified that she had no instructions on what to do if one of the applicants refused to sign prior to hire.)

The hiring practice was initiated by agreement between the company and the union and was followed with the full consent and knowledge of the union.

The Board held that since, in practice, this hiring arrangement required new employees to join the union prior to the expiration of the thirty-day grace period permitted by Taft-Hartley, both company and union were in violation of the Act (*Campbell Soup Co.,* 152 NLRB No. 165).

Some states do not allow contracts to be made containing a union-shop clause, and laws banning such a contract are specifically permitted by the Labor Act (usually any state law which attempts to buck the Labor Act is of no effect). Unless these laws specifically prevent such an agreement—or are so construed by courts or attorneys general—unions try to obtain agency-shop agreements in such states. An agency-shop agreement allows an employee to refuse to join the union but requires that he pay the union a fee equivalent to dues, as compensation for representing him. For, the reasoning goes, if a majority of employees pick a union to represent them, the minority cannot thumb their noses. They stand to share in the gains, and so must help bear the costs.

HOW TO AVOID THE EMPLOYER'S
FIVE CARDINAL SINS

IN THE BEGINNING only the employer could violate the Labor Act. Not until the Taft-Hartley amendments were passed in 1947 did Congress concede that union officers could now and then do things that would obstruct interstate commerce.

Here is the employer's quintalogue of cardinal sins:

(1) Thou shalt not interfere with an employee's Section 7 rights.

(2) Thou shalt not consort with a "company union."

(3) Thou shalt not mistreat employees to encourage or discourage them from joining a union.

(4) Thou shalt not discharge employees for seeking the protection of the Labor Act.

(5) Thou shalt not refuse to bargain in good faith about wages, hours, and other conditions of employment with a union selected by a majority of your employees.

These five "shalt nots" are found in Section 8(a) of the Act, so the sins are known as violations of 8(a)(1), 8(a)(2), 8(a)(3), etc.

Since only the essence of the five commandments is given here —to spare you the legal gobbledygook—one thing must be explained: the first commandment is expressed in such broad terms —forbidding an employer to interfere with, restrain, or coerce employees in the exercise of the rights guaranteed in Section 7—that any violation of the other commandments necessarily involves a violation of the first. Such a transgression is called a "derivative violation" of the first commandment. An employer's conduct may, of course, violate the first and none of the others.

The First Commandment

Any interference, coercion, or restraint by an employer with the Section 7 rights of employees to organize, form, join, or assist a union, to bargain collectively, or to refrain from doing any of these things violates the first. Under the Labor Act, any monkeying around by an employer with his employees' Section 7 rights is an unfair labor practice. Section 7 rights (see page 68) protect the employee's option to act with his fellow employees to set up a union or refrain and be a rugged individualist.

Examples of employer behavior that could be construed to be coercive:

"Mary, there'll be no more overtime if those fellows get in here."

"I tell you, fellows, if that union gets in here this plant will be closed."

"Mike, are you going to vote for that union?"

Making like the FBI and spying or pretending to spy on union gatherings.

Giving the boys an unscheduled raise when you first get wind that there's an organizer snooping around.

Those are rather obvious examples. But some of the decisions pose real problems. Consider these:

Case 1. A trial examiner held that an employer violated the first commandment when he had his office girls, clad in micromini skirts, parade in front of the plant carrying signs reading "Yes on Mini, No on Union" to influence production workers against the union. The Board approved this decision. But a circuit court refused to go along and in effect reversed the Board. It said: "Nowhere in the decision of the Board or the Trial Examiner is there any direct or any implied finding that the activities of the miniskirted clericals was accompanied by any promises of benefits."

Remember this: the Board is not bound by circuit-court decisions; only Supreme Court decisions restrict it.

Case 2. While an election was pending, the company failed to follow its past practice of giving employees a Christmas bonus and merit increases. It informed the employees that union activity was the reason for the refusal to confer the bonus and raises.

The trial examiner held that the company's failure to grant benefits while the election was pending violated the Labor Act. He recommended that the company be ordered to pay the Christmas bonus the employees normally would have received.

> As we understand the law [the trial examiner said], an employer's legal obligation in deciding to grant benefits such as a bonus or wage increases while a union organizational campaign is going on or while an election is pending is to determine and to act on the matter precisely as he would if a union was not in the picture. If the employer would have granted the benefits because of past practice or circumstances unrelated to union activity or a pending election, the grant of such benefits will not violate the Act. But if the employer's course is altered by virtue of the union's presence, then the employer has violated the Act and this is true whether he confers benefits or withholds them because of the union.

He also recommended that "in the event that any employees would have normally received merit wage increases in the period when union activity was taking place and an election was pending," the company should "pay them such merit increases that they normally would have received and make them whole for any loss of merit increases that were not paid because of union activity and the pendency of an election" (*New Fern Restorium*, 180 NLRB No. 95).

The problem presented to management when an election is pending but a wage increase must be granted employees if the company is not to lose its younger employees to competitors is one of the toughest imposed by labor relations law.

It's easy for the Board to say that the employer should do what he normally would have done if the union were not in the picture. But it is difficult if not impossible to prove that a wage increase granted while an NLRB election is pending was not designed to influence votes. In the rare instance where it is the company practice to raise wages at a specified time each year, it may be possible.

How to win. Don't grant the normal increase until after the vote.

Case 3. In *Veeder-Root Co.* (Case No. 6-CA-1520 [1971]), while the union was trying to organize its plant, but before it demanded recognition, the company announced that a consulting firm would conduct a survey of the employees' opinions.

The next day all of the hourly employees, supervisors, weekly salaried personnel, and department managers were divided into small groups, which then took turns going to a conference room where they were required to complete an extensive written questionnaire.

The questionnaire had thirty-six questions, which required the employee to set forth his views on various phases of the company's personnel practices, supervisory policies, and working conditions. Seven of these questions required the employee to write out the answers. The remaining questions were completed by checking an appropriate box. Question 12 required the employee to check a "Help" or "Hurt" box in response to the question "Do you think a union would help or hurt this plant?" No. 13 required the employee to explain, in writing, his answer to the preceding question. No. 23 required the employee to check a "Yes" or "No" box in response to the question "Do you think that a company which treats people fairly and pays well needs a union?" No. 24 required the employee to write out an explanation for the answer given to No. 23.

The questionnaires did not require the employees to give their names. However, the participants were required to write the name of their department or their group number on the first page and indicate whether they were male or female.

Evidence was introduced that some supervisors could identify the handwriting of employees in their departments.

The trial examiner held that the Act had been violated because the safeguards set out by the Board for polling employees in *Struksnes Construction Co., Inc.* (165 NLRB No. 1062) had not been observed. In that case the Board held that in the absence of unusual circumstances a company interrogation of employees will be deemed unlawful unless the following conditions are met:

The purpose is (1) to determine whether to challenge an election, (2) to prepare a defense against an unfair-labor-practice complaint, or (3) to determine the truth of a union's claim of majority.

This purpose is communicated to the employees.

Assurances against reprisal are given.

The company has not engaged in independent conduct which manifests hostility to the union or union organization (which just about begs the question when the purpose of the interrogation is to prepare a defense against a complaint of antiunion conduct!).

Interrogation does not take place when an election is pending.

A circuit court has held that a company that discriminates against some of its employees on account of race violates the first commandment. In its ruling the court concluded that discrimination in favor of white employees and against black employees sets up a clash of interest between whites and blacks which reduces the likelihood that they will act in concert and that such discrimination creates docility in blacks which impedes them from asserting their Section 7 rights. The court made these findings on the authority of psychologist Kenneth C. Clark's 1965 book *Dark Ghetto* and sociologist Gunnar Myrdal's 1944 book *An American Dilemma*.

In substance the court said that more than refusal to bargain with a union was involved in this case: that the very existence of a policy of discrimination in employment on account of race is an unfair labor practice. One of the black employees could have filed an unfair-labor-practice charge even if no union had been on the scene. He could have obtained a cease-and-desist order which could have been enforced by a jail sentence.

In effect the court made the Labor Act another Title VII of the Civil Rights Act of 1964, which expressly forbids discrimination in employment based on race.

To conclude: turn the other cheek if you know an employee is active in sponsoring a union unless he tries to rape one of the girls or you catch him practically stealing the plant!

The Second Commandment

Any attempt by an employer to dominate a union or interfere with the formation of a union by his employees, or any contribution by him to it or in support of it, violates the second commandment.

This stricture is aimed at what are called "company unions." In effect it forbids the boss to sit on both sides of the bargaining table when the parties get down to deciding what he shall pay the employees for their labor. The ban has also been construed to prohibit an employer from helping one union and denying such help to another when two rival unions are seeking to represent his employees. It has been found that when an employer gives privileges to one of two legitimate unions competing for the loyalty of his employees, the employer usually feels he will fare better if the favored union wins representation rights.

If the "union" is the employer's creature, it will be held that he dominates it, by which is meant that he suggests it be started, how it will operate, etc. Indeed in the early days of NLRB, when there were lots of violations of the second commandment, it was not uncommon for representatives of management to take part in the "union's" meetings and try to influence its actions and policies.

Illegal assistance and support is the lesser of this two-headed prohibition. When an employer merely supports a union, the NLRB will tell him to cut it out and not to recognize the favored union until such time as it has been certified by the Board as the representative of the employees; when an employer dominates a union, the NLRB will order the illegal organization put out of existence.

The second commandment is also violated when the employer:

Is active in organizing a "union committee."
Puts the squeeze on the employees to join a union.
Lets Union A solicit employees during working time and denies Union B that privilege.
Has newly hired employees sign union membership applications

accompanied by authorizations to withhold union dues from their wages.

Pays employees for time spent on the assisted union's business.

Employers may, however, pay employees and their union representatives for time spent in discussing a grievance during working hours.

Not too many violations of the second commandment come along these days, perhaps because employees have become more sophisticated. The last big case involving a company union was *NLRB* v. *Cabot Carbon Co.* (360 U.S. 203 [1959]).

The company invited its workers to select a committee to represent them. This was done, and the bylaws drawn up by the committee were approved by the employees. There were no dues, officers, or funds; in fact, no formal organization. Monthly meetings were held with management on company time. Each year the outgoing committee conducted an election of a new committee. Management assisted in holding the elections, calling meetings, preparing minutes, and defraying all expenses of operating the committee.

There was no bargaining. All benefits, privileges, or concessions to employees depended entirely upon the company, even where they grew directly out of a committee request. Over a period of years the committee made recommendations concerning seniority, transfers, job classifications, job bidding, working facilities, vacations, holidays, allocation of company houses, and adjustment of grievances.

This was the mode of operation when a union decided to organize the plant. The union filed an unfair-labor-practice charge claiming that the committee was a company union. It asked the NLRB to order the company to disband the committee. The Board issued the order.

The circuit court agreed that if the committee was a "labor organization" as defined by the Taft-Hartley Act, it was clearly a company union. But the court decided that, whatever the committee was, it was not a labor organization. The Supreme Court reversed the decision, holding that the committee *was* a labor

81

organization and ordering it put out of existence. Committees that deal with management concerning grievances, it ruled, are company unions.

In 1961 the Supreme Court held that an employer violated the second commandment when he and the union entered into an agreement under which the employer recognized the union as the exclusive bargaining representative of his employees although in fact only a minority of the employees had authorized the union to represent them. This was held to be a violation even though the employer had believed in good faith that the union had the consent of the majority of the employees in the appropriate bargaining unit. The recognition was unlawful support of a union (*International Ladies' Garment Workers' Union* v. *NLRB* 366 U.S. 731).

The Third Commandment

Any action or omission by an employer which discriminates against an employee in regard to hiring him or while he is on the job to encourage or discourage membership in a union violates the third. Any discrimination because an employee has refrained from joining a union is also a violation, except where a valid union-shop agreement is in effect (this exception, an important one, was discussed on page 69).

The prime transgression would be firing or otherwise hurting an employee economically because he has engaged in "union activity," i.e., he has been advocating that his fellow employees should unionize. This charge causes a lot of grief because it depends on what went on in the employer's mind when he dismissed the man. The Act permits an employer to discharge for economic reasons or for breach of discipline or for poor workmanship, if those are his *real* reasons. Indeed it has been said that an employer may discharge for a good reason, a bad reason, or no reason at all. But even if there's a good reason, the employer may not discipline or otherwise harass the employee if his hidden but real purpose is to punish him for "pushing" the union. Trial examiners

82

go to great length to find that the given reason for discharging an employee was a mere pretext and that the real reason was because the employer wanted to get rid of a union activist.

Of course, the company cannot be held guilty of discharging a man for union activity if it doesn't know he is so engaged. And that means that no one in management knows he is so engaged, including the lowest-ranking foreman. But even this common-sense rule has an exception: under what is known as the "small-plant theory" an employee's union activities are presumed to be known by the company in a plant with a small work force, even though it does not know he actually is plugging for the union (*Wiese Plow Welding Co., Inc.*, 123 NLRB No. 616).

And if the company knows that an employee is engaged in trying to persuade his fellows to espouse a union and fires him for something outrageous which it thinks in all good faith he has done, but which in fact he has not done, it will also be found guilty. Here is what happened in one case:

"I heard him say he's going to dynamite the plant if the union doesn't win." This was the gist of an affidavit received by an employer concerning Davis, an employee who was known to be agitating for the union. So Davis was fired. But subsequently it turned out that Davis hadn't made the threat.

The NLRB ruled against the employer. It held that "good faith" is no excuse. An employer who disciplines an employee engaged in union activity is guilty of trying to discourage union membership unless he can prove that the misconduct actually occurred.

However, every now and then the Board will approve the discharge of a union activist when one would swear the employer's motivation was to discourage such activity rather than to punish for an infraction. Here's a rather amusing example:

This happened in Chicago. A company's North Side salesmen and its South Side salesmen were having a joint picnic. Wives and kids were there, too. The refreshments were not limited to soft drinks. The climax of the day was to be a softball game between the North and the South. In the delicate language of the NLRB,

"Competition was quite intense, as the participants had wagered $10 per person on the outcome of the game." Like the old Dodgers and the Giants; or the old Yankees and the Red Sox.

Cooksley was pitching for the North Side. He kept riding Simmons (not Al), who was playing first base for the South Side. When Simmons went to the plate Cooksley would bellow, "Get your foot out of the bucket, yellow" . . . "Stop picking your nose in front of the kids" . . . "Simmons is a pianist," etc. Cooksley was yanked in the fifth. The tirade went on from the bench.

By the eighth inning Simmons had had it. He turned and yelled at Cooksley, "After the third out I'm coming after you." (Note the devotion to baseball—after the third out!)

With the third out, Simmons walked over to Cooksley and Cooksley bit the dust.

After the game Simmons and Cooksley shook hands. But there was a company rule prohibiting fighting, and Simmons had taken part in a recent fruitless attempt to organize the salesmen. The company fired Simmons.

Surprise: the Board dismissed a complaint by the union that the company had violated the third commandment (*Nehi-Royal Crown Corporation*, 178 NLRB No. 19).

It is a heavy burden to prove that your motive is pure when you discharge an employee while union activity is going on in your plant. It's so heavy, in fact, that if you know that the employee is pushing unionization it would probably be just as well to overlook minor infractions of discipline. In such a situation, it is almost impossible to prove that your motive for firing an employee was not adulterated by a desire to get rid of a union "agitator."

Other examples of violations of the third commandment include:

Refusing to reinstate an economic striker who has offered unconditionally to return to work when a job he is qualified to do is open, or even failing to let him know that the job is open.

Discharging the employees after they "go union" and then opening a plant elsewhere to perform the same operations with nonunion employees. (The latter plant is known as a "runaway plant.")

Refusing to hire a person because he belongs to a union, does not belong to a union, or belongs to Union X instead of Union Y.

Denying vacation pay to strikers while granting it to nonstrikers.

The Fourth Commandment

Discharging or otherwise discriminating against an employee because he has filed charges or given testimony under the Labor Act violates the fourth commandment. Violations of it are in most cases also violations of the third.

Examples include refusing to reinstate an employee when a job is open for which he is qualified because he filed charges with the NLRB claiming his layoff was based on union activity; and demoting an employee because he testified at a Board hearing or gave affidavits to a Board investigator.

The Fifth Commandment

This one seems simple; it merely says that an employer may not refuse to bargain with a union selected by a majority of his employees. But it is the most complicated of all. The reason is that the Labor Act defines what is meant by "to bargain." And, on top of that, two rules have been added—the *Borg-Warner* rules (below) and the *Fibreboard rule* (see page 125).

The Act's definition of "to bargain," which applies to both companies and unions, is found in Section 8(d), which says in part: that the employer and the union must meet at reasonable intervals and confer in good faith about wages, hours, and other terms and conditions of employment or negotiate an agreement on any question arising under such an agreement [but neither party has to agree to a proposal by the other or make a concession!]; and that if one party so requests, the other party must sign a written instrument incorporating the terms agreed upon.

Thus oral labor contracts are perfectly good, though they are rare indeed.

Unfortunately, the definition doesn't stop there, as though the problem of whether a party is conferring in good faith doesn't cause enough headaches, since it means determining what is going on within someone's head. No, the definition goes on to include the rituals that have to be performed if there is currently in effect a written labor contract and one of the parties wants to change or terminate it. In such a case that party must:

Serve a written notice of what he wants to do sixty days prior to the expiration date of the current contract.

Offer to meet and confer with the other party for the purpose of negotiating a new contract.

Notify the federal and state agencies charged with trying to get parties to agree to a new contract rather than resort to strike or lockout within thirty days of the notice.

Live up to the terms of the current contract for sixty days after giving the notice or until the expiration date of the current contract, whichever occurs later.

Finally, the definition includes a clause that says an employee who strikes within the sixty-day period loses the protection of the Act.

The Borg-Warner rules: On top of all these rules, the Supreme Court in 1958 established what are known as the *Borg-Warner* rules. There are, the court said, three separate categories of bargaining subjects: mandatory, permissible, and illegal.

Mandatory subjects are wages, hours, and other terms and conditions of employment. On such subjects as how much the raise will be, how many hours a day the employees must work, how long the contract will run, and hundreds of others, you must bargain in good faith. But you don't have to give in to what the union demands. When you and the union reach the point where it is obvious that neither of you is going to budge (called point of impasse) and the union calls the men out on strike, the strike will be called an economic strike. This means you can replace the strikers permanently with new employees. It also means that when the strikers give up, you cannot be ordered to pay them for the time they didn't work. (Don't laugh. If employees go out on strike because you are not bargaining in good faith, they are called "unfair-labor-

86

practice strikers," and if they give in and unconditionally ask for their jobs, you have to reinstate them and pay them for the time they didn't work!)

Permissible subjects are negotiable matters not strictly related to wages, hours, or terms and conditions of employment; for example, a demand by you that the contract include a clause that employees must vote on your final offer before they strike, or a demand by the union that you spend x amount of dollars in advertising during the next year. You must not push these subjects to impasse, for if you do and the union strikes, the strike will be labeled an unfair-labor-practice strike.

Illegal subjects violate the Act. Examples of an illegal subject would be a demand by the employer not to have to recognize a certified union as the exclusive bargaining agent of the employees in the unit, or a demand by the union that it be allowed to strike inside the sixty-day period mentioned above.

Bargaining in good faith: The Labor Act does not require agreement. What is required is that the parties come to the bargaining table

to enter into discussion with an open and fair mind, and a sincere purpose to find a basis of agreement . . . The employer may have either good or bad reasons, or no reason at all, for instance on the inclusion or exclusion of a proposed contract term. If the insistence is genuinely and sincerely held, if it is not mere window dressing, it may be maintained forever though it produce a stalemate . . . On the other hand, while the employer is assured these valuable rights, he may not use them as a cloak . . . it takes more than mere "surface bargaining" or "shadow-boxing to a draw" or "giving the union a runaround while purporting to be meeting with the union for the purpose of collective bargaining" [*NLRB v. Herman Sausage Co.*, 275 F.2d 229].

Quite obviously your conduct in the past must be consistent with an adamant stand in the present. Thus if you deny a union-shop clause when a union is negotiating for such a clause in your office-workers unit, because, you assert, you are opposed to requiring anyone to have to join a union to keep his job, yet your production people have a union-shop clause in their contract, your good faith will be suspect. Or if you oppose the withholding of union dues because of the nuisance and expense but in the past you have deducted contributions as authorized by your employees for the United Fund, a similar conclusion may well be reached. But you can say, "I'm not going to grant a ten percent wage increase come hell or high water" and you will be protected. (Just don't say "I can't afford it" or you will be called on to prove it.)

A trial examiner has held a company guilty of failure to bargain in good faith because over a period of a year only ten bargaining sessions with the union were held due to the fact that the company's spokesman was a lawyer who had so much business that every time a bargaining session was scheduled he would have to call it off to attend to something or other for another client!

The trial examiner said: "The Company failed to display the degree of diligence that proper performance of its bargaining obligation required. This is so—whether or not delays were inspired by a deliberate scheme to engage in dilatory tactics. Although the Company attorney's situation in having other business to take care of besides that of the Company may be sympathized with, nevertheless it was the duty of the Company to see to it that if [the attorney] was not available, a substitute should be appointed so that the bargaining meetings need not be postponed on so many occasions" (A. W. Thompson, Inc., Case 16-CA-3683 [1970]).

In another case, an impasse had been reached on three union demands—more holidays, a vacation bonus, and company agreement to check off union dues. Bargaining broke off. Six months later the union softened its demands on the first two issues but stated in a letter that it was adamant about the checkoff. The company believed that the checkoff was the key and that impasse would result again. It thought that holding another bargaining session would merely be going through futile motions. The Board stated that the union's modified proposal if granted would place a substantially smaller economic burden on the company. This, it held, despite the union's refusal to budge on the checkoff issue, was enough to break the impasse and restore the obligation to bargain. Thus the fifth commandment was violated by the company's refusal to resume bargaining (*Webb Furniture Co.,* 152 NLRB No. 160).

The Supreme Court has held that if a company grants a wage increase during negotiations but before impasse has been reached, it has not bargained in good faith (*NLRB* v. *Katz,* 396 U.S. 736). But that court has also held that if an impasse has been reached, a company may grant an increase but not of a greater amount than offered the union (*NLRB* v. *Crompton Highland Mills,* 377 U.S. 217).

How to win. Notify the union that you intend to grant an increase because the negotiations have been running too long and you have to keep your employees from quitting and getting work elsewhere. Tell the union the amount of the raise you intend to put into effect. Tell the employees that the union is not satisfied and that you stand ready to continue bargaining on wages.

The 60-day-notice requirement. The contract expired at midnight, 12:01 A.M., January 5, 1970. The contract was automatically renewed for another year unless the party desiring to change or terminate the contract notified the other party in writing sixty days prior to the expiration date.

The union notice was postmarked in Casper, Wyoming, on the afternoon of November 5, 1969. It was sent by certified mail and addressed to the company's president in Billings, Montana, P.O. Box 2516. The envelope was stamped in Billings "Notified November 6, 1969."

A trial examiner refused to find the company guilty of refusing to bargain, because the company had received the letter somewhere between eight and seventeen hours late for the full sixty-day notice to be effective. Consequently the strike that followed the refusal to bargain was not an unfair-labor-practice strike.

The date of receipt, not the date of mailing, is where you start counting. And a notice is received when it is deposited at the addressee's post-office box or office or residence, as the case may be. This is how the trial examiner counted: "There are four days in January, 1970, thirty-one days in December, 1969, and twenty-five days in November, 1969, giving a total of 60 days at 12:01 A.M., November 6, 1969. A 60-day notice would have to have been deposited in the Company's box prior to midnight, 12:01 A.M., November 6, 1969. As the notification was not placed in the Company's post office box until after that hour and at some time on November 6, 1969, a 60-day notice was not given" (*Sawyer Stores, Inc.*, Case No. 27-CA-2926 [1971]).

The Board adopted a trial examiner's holding that a union had violated Section 8(b)(5) under the following circumstances. During the term of the contract a steward notified the company that all the union members would attend a rally the next day from 11:30 A.M. to 1:30 P.M. and that the rally would pertain to amending the contract with the company and other employers to raise the minimum wage to $100. The normal lunch period was from 11:45 to 12:45. The company protested that such absence would break the "no strike" clause in the contract.

Nevertheless, the next day 150 employees left the premises and did not return until sometime between 1:45 and 2:30 P.M. During that time the union's president addressed the crowd, making a vigorous plea for a $100 minimum weekly wage and urging resort, if necessary, to work stoppages to achieve that goal.

The NLRB held that while the strike was of relatively short duration, Section 8(d) does not distinguish between short strikes and long strikes. The union violated it and violated its obligation to bargain in good faith (*Melville Shoe Corporation*, 187 NLRB, No. 107).

How far the Borg-Warner rule may go. The Board has held that retirees and pensioners are employees within the meaning of that word as defined in the Labor Act. Accordingly, the company's refusal to bargain with their former union concerning changes in their retirement benefits is an unfair labor practice.

Under the collective-bargaining agreement, at the date Medicare became effective the company was paying two dollars a month per retiree for medical and surgical insurance. The company believed that a "nonduplication-of-benefits clause" in the insurance policy made the coverage redundant to the extent that benefits were provided by Medicare.

Over the protests of the union representing current employees, the company offered retired employees the option of continuing the insurance or electing to have the company pay a three-dollar-per-month premium for a voluntary insurance plan under Medicare Part B, supplementing that statute's hospital plan by providing for the payment of doctors' bills.

The trial examiner recommended that the union's complaint be dismissed on the ground that retirees are not "employees" as defined in the Act. The Board reversed and ordered the company to rescind payment of the three dollars per month on behalf of the 15 out of 190 retirees who had elected the second option (*Pittsburgh Plate Glass Co.*, 177 NLRB No. 114).

The circuit court refused to enforce the Board's order that the company bargain. It not only thought that persons who have retired are not "employees" but also that they are no longer in the bargaining unit. Thus, the court held, the company did not violate the fifth commandment when it refused to bargain.

The Supreme Court has agreed to review this case. It is improbable that it will agree with the Board, but if it does a veritable Pandora's box will be opened and the following problems fly out:

The Board argues that changes in retirement benefits "affect the availability of employer funds available for active employees" and that therefore such changes should be mandatory subjects of bargaining. But all management salaries and indeed all dividends and capital expenditures affect the availability of employer funds for active employees. Should such outlays be mandatory subjects of bargaining?

The Board argues that many companies, such as the big steel and auto concerns, have agreed in collective bargaining to pay more liberal pensions to already retired employees. Does this mean that if many companies voluntarily bargain about a subject, that subject suddenly becomes a mandatory subject of bargaining?

If retired employees are considered members of the bargaining unit, shouldn't they have the right to vote for union officers and the obligation to pay dues? Shouldn't they have the right to vote in NLRB representation and decertification elections?

Won't the unions have to worry about lawsuits and NLRB complaints by the oldsters claiming unfair representation?

The Board went to great length in its opinion to prove that Americans are retiring earlier and living longer. It could happen that eventually a company might have more retired employees than active ones. Wouldn't that be a pretty kettle of fish?

If the retirees chose Union A as their bargaining representative when they were active, but now Union B represents the active employees, which union should now represent the retirees?

Would the union be inclined to "trade off" the benefits of retirees for additional benefits for active members? (The late, great Walter P. Reuther did just the opposite.)

II

SOME THINGS YOU CAN PREVENT
UNIONS FROM DOING

IT'S HARD TO believe today, but from 1935 to 1947, when the late Senator Taft's "slave labor law" was passed amending the Wagner Act, unions could do no wrong under the Labor Act. The Taft-Hartley Act not only put a stop to this but even condemned more actions by unions than were included in the employer's quintalogue.

Here they are in brief (and brief is the word for it, since there was so much pulling and hauling in the Congress that passed the Taft-Hartley Act that some of the language is confusing and after twenty-five years there are still clauses that remain obscure):

Under Section 8(b)(1)(A), a union must not restrain employees in the exercise of their Section 7 rights (see page 68).

Under Section 8(b)(1)(B), a union must not restrain or coerce an employer in the selection of his bargaining representative.

Under Section 8(b)(2), a union must not cause an employer to discriminate against an employee in violation of the employer's third commandment (see pages 82 and 83).

Under Section 8(b)(3), a union must not refuse to bargain in good faith with a company about wages, hours, and other conditions of employment if it is the representative of his employees.

Under Section 8(b)(4), a union must not engage in strikes or boycotts to accomplish certain "objects" (see page 109).

Under Section 8(b)(5), a union must not require an employee covered by a union security contract to pay an excessive initiation fee in order to join the union.

Under Section 8(b)(6), a union must not cause or attempt to

cause an employer to pay for services not performed or not to be performed (called "featherbedding").

Under Section 8(b)(7) (added in 1959 by Landrum-Griffin, rather than by Taft-Hartley), a union that is not certified as the employees' representative may not engage in picketing to force an employer to recognize it as representative of his employees irrespective of what the employees wish (see page 97).

And now, in more detail:

Section 8(b)(1)(A): It will be recalled that violations of the employer's second through fifth commandments "derivatively" violate the employer's first commandment, which forbids interference with an employee's Section 7 rights. But the Board has held that Section 8(b)(1)(A) is not derivatively violated when any of the other 8(b) admonitions to unions are violated. There's one exception: making or enforcing illegal union security agreements or hiring agreements that condition employment on union membership not only violates Section 8(b)(2) but violates Section 8(b)(1)(A) as well. Such action restrains or coerces employees in the exercise of their Section 7 rights.

This section also bans any union conduct designed to cause nonstriking employees to refuse to cross the picket line, even if it doesn't succeed. Remember, one of the employees' Section 7 rights is that of refraining from assisting a union.

Examples of the sort of rough stuff that violates the section would be:

Threatening a nonstriker with loss of his job if the union gets majority backing.

Blocking the entrance to the plant with bodies so a nonstriker cannot go into work.

Throwing a rock through the windshield of a nonstriker's car.

"We'll get you, you scab!"

Agreeing with an employer that the union shall be recognized as the exclusive representative of the employees when it has not been chosen by a majority of the employees.

How to win. File a charge in the nearest regional office. Remember, anyone may file a charge to set the NLRB machinery moving. He may be just a citizen observing the rough stuff and have no immediate interest in the situation. Ask the Regional Director to seek a 10(J) injunction.

Section 8(b)(1)(B): This one bans restraints on the employer in picking his bargaining agent and applies whether or not the union represents a majority of the employees.

For instance, the section is violated if the union refuses to bargain with a labor relations attorney representing the company and demands that a company executive do the negotiation, or if it strikes individual members of a multi-employer bargaining unit and thus obtains individual contracts instead of one contract covering all the members of the unit.

Section 8(b)(2): This one forbids a union to cause an employer to break the employer's third commandment by discriminating against an employee in regard to wages, hours, or employment conditions to encourage or discourage membership in a union. It does not allow a union to cause an employer to discriminate against an employee to the extent that the union can demand that an employer fire an employee who has not joined the union.

This kind of encouragement to join the union is permitted when a valid union security agreement is in effect (see page 69). Union security agreements that do not meet the requirement of making compulsory membership valid will not support a discharge by the employer caused by the union. Section 8(b)(2) is also violated when a union tries to force an employer to enter an illegal union security agreement.

Contracts or informal arrangements with a union under which an employer gives preferential treatment to union members are violations of Section 8(b)(2). It is not unlawful for an employer and a union to enter an agreement whereby the employer agrees to hire new employees exclusively through the union hiring hall so long as there is neither a provision in the agreement, nor a practice in effect, that discriminates against nonunion members in favor of union members. Both the agreement and the actual operation of the hiring hall must be nondiscriminatory; referrals must be made without reference to union membership.

Examples of violations of Section 8(b)(2) are: Causing an employer to discharge an employee because he circulated a petition urging a change in the union's method of selecting shop stewards; causing an employer to discharge an employee because he made speeches against a contract proposed by the union; and making a contract that requires an employer to hire only members of the union or employees "satisfactory" to the union.

Section 8(b)(3): This is the union's counterpart of the employer's fifth commandment. A union must not refuse to bargain in good faith with an employer about wages, hours, and other conditions of employment if it is the representative of his employees.

It is a violation of this section for a union to strike an employer to compel him to bargain separately if in the past he has bargained on a multi-employer basis. The multi-employer bargaining rules are considered at page 177.

Section 8(b)(4): This is the boycott ban (see page 109).

Section 8(b)(5): It is illegal for a union to charge employees who are covered by an authorized union security agreement a membership fee "in an amount which the Board finds excessive or discriminatory under all the circumstances." The section also provides that the Board in making its finding must consider among other factors "the practices and customs of labor organizations in the particular industry, and the wages currently paid to the employees affected."

Examples of violations of this section include: charging old employees who do not join the union until after a union security agreement goes into effect an initiation fee of $15 while charging new employees only $5; and increasing the initiation fee from $75 to $250 and thus charging new members an amount equal to about four weeks' wages when other unions in the area charge a fee equal to about one-half the employee's first week's pay.

Section 8(b)(6): A labor organization is forbidden "to cause or attempt to cause an employer to pay or deliver or agree to pay or deliver any money or other thing of value, in the nature of an exaction, for services which are not performed or not to be performed." In other words, this section prohibits practices commonly known as featherbedding.

This stricture is practically a dead letter. It has been held that even though he doesn't want work done, an employer cannot charge a violation of the section and make it stick if he agrees that it shall be done and paid for.

Section 8(b)(7): Added to the Labor Act in 1959, this section is aimed at "blackmail picketing." This is how a sponsor of the 1959 amendments described blackmail picketing to the House of Representatives:

It is intended to prohibit blackmail recognition picketing by unions which do not represent the employees. Under the National Labor Relations Act elaborate election machinery is provided for ascertaining the wishes of employees in selecting or rejecting bargaining representatives. The Act contains provisions for giving employees an opportunity to vote by secret ballot. In recent years the safeguards intended by these election provisions have been thwarted by unions which have lost elections and unions which do not have enough employee support to petition for an election but yet insist upon compelling employers to sign contracts with them—irrespective of the sentiment of the employees.

The customary method employed to force employers to do this is to place picket lines around their plants or shops. Such picketing, even when peaceful, will frequently cause small employers to capitulate. The picket line is a signal for truckers not to pick up or deliver goods to employees of maintenance contractors. Pickets also deter many customers from entering retail or service establishments. In the face of such tactics employees whose jobs are in jeopardy as they see their employer's business blocked off are soon coerced into joining the picketing union—even though they might prefer another union. In many such cases their employer forces them in a particular union by signing a compulsory membership agreement with the picketing union.

The NLRB has attempted to give some relief to employers and employees victimized in such situations by holding it an unfair labor practice for a union to picket for recognition after it has lost an election.

While such relief seems called for, nevertheless the courts of appeal are in conflict as to whether the Board has even this limited power [105 *Congressional Record* 14347 (1959)].

Section 8(b)(7) is as complicated as the one barring boycotts. Boiled down, this is it:

If recognition is an object, peaceful picketing is forbidden when there is a valid contract with another union; when an election has been held in the past twelve months; or after a reasonable time—not more than thirty days—has passed without an election petition having been filed.

Picketing to inform the public is permitted unless recognition is also an object or deliveries are interrupted.

The NLRB is required to go into the federal district court and seek an injunction to stop the picketing if the Regional Director's preliminary investigation of a company's charge finds reasonable evidence that Section 8(b)(7) has been violated.

But the Board has knocked holes in the protection the section was supposed to have given. Thus it has held that if one object of the picketing is to inform the public that you don't employ union members or that you have no contract with the picketing union, the fact that another objective is to force you to recognize the union doesn't make the picketing a violation (*Crown Cafeteria,* 135 NLRB No. 124).

If the words on the picket signs are cleverly chosen, you probably cannot do a thing unless the picketing causes the stoppage of deliveries. However, the Board has even held that picketing was legal where the signs said the employer paid substandard wages *even though deliveries were stopped.* It said that such "union standards" picketing is not picketing for recognition (*Claude Everett Construction Co.,* 136 NLRB No. 28).

The Board has also held that a majority union would be justified in picketing after the thirty-day limit if it filed a refusal-to-bargain charge that was found to be valid (*C. A. Blinne Construction Co.,* 135 NLRB No. 121).

When such a charge is filed, the company can get a "quickie" election unless the Regional Director finds that the picketing is for the purpose of truthfully advising the public that an employer does not employ union members or have a contract with a union. Even that loophole closes if the effect of the picketing induces truck drivers to refuse to drive through the line and make deliveries.

12

HOW TO AVOID BARGAINING WITH A
UNION YOUR EMPLOYEES DON'T WANT

ALTHOUGH THE LABOR ACT in Section 9(c) seems to require that a union with which an employer has the duty to bargain must have been selected in an election by a secret ballot, the NLRB has managed to gain Supreme Court approval of a doctrine which requires an employer to bargain with a union although no election has been held or even if an election has been held and the union lost it.

In brief, this doctrine holds that if a majority of employees in an appropriate bargaining unit sign cards authorizing the union to represent them and the employer commits unfair labor practices or, not committing unfair labor practices, concedes that the union does represent a majority, the NLRB can order the employer to bargain with the union.

Since many people will sign just about anything if urged to do so by their fellows, it often happens that a majority of employees will sign cards and if an election is held the union will lose. The reason, of course, is that many who signed the cards showed their true sentiments in the secrecy of the polling booth.

From the name of the case in which the Supreme Court approved it in 1969, the doctrine is known as the *Gissel* doctrine (*NLRB* v. *Gissel Packing Co.*, 395 U.S. 575).

The doctrine had its origins back in 1964. The Textile Workers Union held signed authorization cards from fifty-three of the company's eighty-eight production and maintenance employees and requested recognition. The company stated that it didn't believe the union had authorization cards from a majority of employees. The union suggested that the cards be turned over to a clergyman for verification. The company refused (even though a veteran employee vouched for the union), stating that it would not recognize the union without an election. The Board held that the company's conduct constituted a refusal to bargain. It was ordered to bargain with the union (*Bernel Foam Products Co.,* 146 NLRB No. 161).

The theory was that the employer was acting in bad faith when he refused to recognize the union. The doctrine was extended to hold that if the employer concurrently committed unfair labor practices (like firing somebody for trying to get cards signed), he was deemed to have a bad-faith doubt about the union's majority status.

In the *Gissel* opinion Chief Justice Earl Warren said that the Board at the argument of the case had abandoned the "bad-faith doubt" theory. He said: "The key to the issuance of a bargaining order is the commission of serious unfair labor practices that interfere with the election processes and tend to preclude the holding of a fair election." However, the chief justice also indicated that the Board was correct when it ruled that an employer could not refuse to bargain if he *knew,* through a personal poll for instance, that a majority of his employees supported the union.

The NLRB General Counsel must show that the company has committed serious unfair labor practices. Here, then, are the present rules concerning the right of the NLRB to order a company to bargain with a union without an election being held or in spite of the fact that a union has lost an election:

The company must have committed "outrageous" or "pervasive" unfair labor practices, in which case the union's demand to bargain need not be proved by the General Counsel, although he must still prove that the union held authorization cards from a majority of employees (*Loray Company,* 184 NLRB No. 27); or the company must have committed "less pervasive" unfair labor practices, which nevertheless tend to undermine majority strength and impede the election processes—in which case, however, a demand to bargain must be proved. "It is for the Board and *not* the courts to make that determination based on its expert estimate as to the effects on the election process of unfair labor practices of varying intensity" (*Gissel*). [This means there's no way of predicting whether certain unfair labor practices are "pervasive" or "less pervasive" or even "minor."]

The bargaining unit proposed by the union must be appropriate.

Authorization cards signed by a majority of the employees in the unit must be held by the union on the day the demand for recognition is made, and these cards must be "countable."

Cards are not countable if the employee's signature is a forgery or was obtained by duress, or if the card merely grants the union authority to seek an election. But a card is countable even though:

It has a dual purpose, i.e., it authorizes the union both to seek an election and to represent the employee who has signed.

It is ambiguous on its face, for example, if the language is such that it could be interpreted to mean that the card authorizes the union to act for the employee only to petition for an election.

The union organizer misrepresents the purpose for which the card is to be used, unless it can be proved that the organizer told the employee who signs the card that the *only* purpose of the card was to obtain an election. This is called the *Cumberland* rule, from *Cumberland Shoe Co.* (144 NLRB No. 1268), and was approved by *Gissel*. The court said that employees "should be bound by the clear language of what they sign." (Carrying this permission to the limit, the Board holds that a card is countable even if the employee can't read English!)

NOTE: The Supreme Court in *Gissel* also said: "There is still a third category, of minor or less extensive unfair labor practices, which because of their minimal impact on the election machinery will not sustain a bargaining order."

How to win. At the first indication that organizing is going on, call in all the supervisors and warn them that they must lean over backward not to commit an unfair labor practice. They must avoid disciplining employees who are "pushing" the union, if that is at all possible. They should be careful not to utter threats or hint about benefits forthcoming if the union is rejected. They should be blind to any soliciting of authorization cards. They should say nothing critical of the union or of unions in general. *Above all be calm &*

collected

You and the supervisors should be alert to any indication that the union is using pressure tactics to persuade employees to sign cards. Get a copy of the card. If its language is ambiguous, try to get proof that the organizers are telling the employees that the cards are to be used *only* to enable the union to petition for an election (the Board requires a 30 percent showing of interest before it will order that an election be held).

When the demand for recognition is made, take some time before answering it. You have the right to interrogate employees about their wishes if this is done in the proper way. (The Board has said: "Questioning was conducted for the purpose of ascertaining whether the union represented a majority of the employees, which purpose was communicated to the employees [who] were assured that the company 'didn't care which way [they] wanted to go,' and the questioning was conducted against a background free of any evidence of hostility to the union and absent the commission of any unfair labor practices" [*Briggs IGA Foodliner*, 146 NLRB No. 393]).

When the organizer offers the cards, refuse to touch them. Make him take them away. You don't have to give a reason. Just tell him to get himself an election. *Don't* make antiunion statements to the organizer.

One possible exception to the above rules may be developing. The Warren Court more or less shoved the NLRB's "bargaining order" rules down the throats of the circuit courts, prompting a Second Circuit judge to remark, "This 'representation' card business is an abomination" (*Scharzenbach Huber Company* v. *NLRB*, 408 F.2d 236).

So there may be a tendency among the circuit courts to water down the entire doctrine, perhaps aided by the "Nixon Board." Here's an example:

The Eighth Circuit Court has held that the NLRB was not warranted in issuing a bargaining order where the union obtained the majority of the authorization cards *after* the company committed unfair labor practices. The time sequence ran as follows: (1) the company interrogated employees and fired a union activist for what the NLRB found to be a pretext (he had said "I think it's a lot of crap" in front of an innocent secretary during a paycheck controversy); (2) the union succeeded in obtaining authorization cards from a majority of the employees; (3) the company fired another union activist for what the NLRB found to be a pretext (drinking on the job) but which the court labeled a justifiable cause; (4) the Board ordered the company to bargain with the union.

In determining whether or not to enforce NLRB bargaining orders as a remedy for independent unfair labor practices, the court divided its post-*Gissel* decisions into three categories:

Where the underlying facts affirmatively show that the unfair labor practices have in fact undermined a union majority, typically evidenced by the union losing an election or the employees seeking to withdraw from the union following the occurrence of the conduct in question, we grant enforcement;

Where the record is silent concerning the actual impact of the employer's unfair labor practices, we defer to the Board's exercise of discretion and grant enforcement; and

Where the evidence establishes that the unfair labor practices produced little or no impact upon the employees' allegiance to the union, we deny enforcement.

The court held that the present case fell into the third category. "Here the organization drive proceeded at an accelerated pace *following* the employer's commission of prohibited practices" (*Arbie Mineral Feed Co.*, 76 LRRM 2613).

In the following case the Board held that the company's unfair labor practice was "minor" and ordered a second election rather than ordering the company to bargain.

In 1968 the company, which had more than seventy plants nationwide, many of them unionized, built a new plant. The management concept in effect at the new plant was "participative management." This approach involved the theory that people are basically honest and that they derive satisfaction from achievement. A crucial aspect of the approach was effective communication between management and employees. Maintaining competitive working conditions, pay, and benefits was also part of the management approach.

A booklet was given new employees describing the foregoing theory and describing the fringe benefits. Employees were urged to communicate readily so that management could learn of "misunderstandings and dissatisfactions . . . and take prompt corrective action if needed" (a grievance procedure).

The union arrived in March 1969. Prior thereto the plant manager had held meetings regularly with the employees and made changes in equipment and policies as suggested by the employees, i.e., adjusted their grievances.

He also did so after the union appeared. These adjustments were held unfair labor practices by the trial examiner, citing *Texaco, Inc.* (178 NLRB No. 72).

The company also said to the employees in a letter, after setting forth the existing benefits: "We stress that all benefits would be negotiated from scratch if a union represented you. Remember! Only Olin Conductors can guarantee you the above benefits."

This, the trial examiner held, was not protected free speech under Section 8(c). It implied the possible loss of existing benefits if the plant "went union" and conversely the continuation of existing benefits if the plant opposed the union.

The trial examiner recommended that the company be ordered to bargain with the union. He held that the Supreme Court's *Gissel* decision (approving bargaining orders based on card counts) means that if a company commits unfair labor practices of significant importance after being presented with valid cards signed by a majority of employees in the unit and the union loses a subsequent election, the Board must order the company to bargain rather than order a rerun election unless it can find that an election "would definitely be the more reliable test of the employees' desires than the card count taken before the unfair labor practice occurred."

Reversing the trial examiner and ordering a rerun election, the Board said: "We do not think that the unfair labor practices herein warrant either a refusal-to-bargain finding based on the union's cards, or the issuance of a bargaining order, under the standards set forth by the Supreme Court in *NLRB* v. *Gissel Packing Co.,* 395 U.S. 575. In our view, the 8(a)(1) violations are neither so extensive in nature nor so pervasive in character as to preclude the holding of a fair rerun election" (*Olin Conductors, Olin Mathieson Chemical Corporation*, 185 NLRB No. 56).

13

BOYCOTTING—WHAT IT IS
AND HOW TO DEAL WITH IT

NO PROBLEM OF labor relations is more acute, complex, or confused than the attempt by Congress to restrict the power unions exert by means of the secondary boycott.

The origin of the word is interesting. A Captain Charles Boycott was agent for the estates of the Earl of Erne in County Mayo during Queen Victoria's reign. In 1880 he refused to receive rents at figures fixed by the tenants. Captain Boycott's life was threatened, his servants were compelled to leave him, his fences were torn down, and his food supplies were interfered with. It took a force of 900 soldiers to protect him. The term "boycott" spread throughout Europe.

The boycotting of the captain was a case of "primary" boycott, but in the United States unions have adopted a different kind: they put pressure on neutral parties to persuade them to stop doing business with the primary party with whom they have a dispute.

Now you'd think all Congress would have had to do was decree that it was illegal for a union to strike innocent A when its real dispute was with that blackguard B. But alas, Congress is made up mostly of lawyers. The statute doesn't even use the word "boycott." It is expressed in such a maze of words that judges are constantly getting lost in it.

Section 8(b)(4)(B) contains the Act's secondary-boycott provision. A secondary boycott occurs if a union has a dispute with Company A and in furtherance of that dispute causes the employees of Company B to stop handling the products of Company A or otherwise forces Company B to stop doing business with

Company A. The dispute is with Company A, called the "primary" employer; the union's action is against Company B, called the "secondary" employer, hence the term "secondary boycott." In many cases the secondary employer is a customer or supplier of the primary employer. In general, the act prohibits both the secondary boycott and the threat of it. Examples of prohibited secondary boycotts are:

Picketing an employer to force him to stop doing business with another employer who has refused to recognize the union.

Asking the employees of a plumbing contractor not to work on connecting air-conditioning equipment manufactured by a nonunion employer whom the union is attempting to organize.

Urging employees of a building contractor not to install doors which were made by a manufacturer which is nonunion or which employs members of a rival union.

Telling an employer that his plant will be picketed if he continues to do business with an employer whom the union has designated as "unfair."

The prohibitions of Section 8(b)(4)(B) do not protect a secondary employer from the incidental effects of union action taken directly against the primary employer. Thus it is lawful for a union to urge employees of a supplier at the primary employer's plant not to cross a picket line there. Nor does the section proscribe union action to prevent an employer from contracting out work customarily performed by his own employees, even though an incidental effect of such conduct might be to compel the employer to cease doing business with the subcontractor.

In order to be protected against the union actions prohibited under this subparagraph, the secondary employer has to be neutral in the dispute between the union and the primary employer. For secondary-boycott purposes an employer is considered an "ally" of the primary employer and therefore not protected from union action in certain situations. One criterion is based on the operational relationship between the primary and secondary employers. Here, a number of factors are considered, particularly the following: Are the primary and secondary employers owned and controlled by the same person or persons? Are they engaged in "closely integrated operations?" May they be treated as a single employer under the Act?

Another test of the ally relationship is based on the conduct of the secondary employer. If an employer, despite his claim of neutrality in the dispute, acts in a way that indicates that he has abandoned his neutral position, he opens himself up to primary action by the union. An example of this would be a contractor who, claiming to be a neutral, enters into an arrangement with a struck employer whereby he accepts farmed-out work from that employer which normally the employer would do himself but cannot perform because his plant is closed by a strike.

The Board has held that B was not an ally of A and that picketing B violated Section 8(b)(4)(B) under the following circumstances. The union began an economic strike against A. There was a warehouse on A's premises where it received supplies for manufacture. Prior to the strike 80 percent of the supplies arrived by truck, the remainder by railroad. After the strike began, A continued to operate the warehouse with salaried employees not in the bargaining unit.

Since truck drivers would not go through the union's picket line, A made an arrangement with B (located two miles away) whereby all truck deliveries originally destined for A were diverted to B. The employees of B merely transferred the supplies from the trucks to railroad cars and the railroad then delivered the cars to A. No supplies were stored by B. The union began to picket B.

In finding that the union had violated Section 8(b)(4)(B) the Board rejected the union's argument that B was an ally of A because the arrangement enabled A to counter the effectiveness of the picket line at A's plant (*Sterling Drug, Inc.*, 189 NLRB No. 11).

When employees of a primary employer and those of a secondary employer work on the same premises, a special situation is involved and the usual rules do not apply. A typical example of the shared-site, or "common situs," situation is where a subcontractor with whom a union has a dispute is engaged at work on a construction site alongside other subcontractors, with whom the union has no dispute. Picketing at a common situs is permissible if directed solely against the primary employer. But it is prohibited if directed against secondary employers regularly engaged at that site.

To assist in determining whether picketing at a common site is restricted to the primary employer and therefore permissible, or directed at a secondary employer and therefore violative of the statute, the NLRB and the courts have suggested various guidelines for evaluating the objective of the picketing. Subject to the qualification noted below, the picketing would appear to be primary picketing if it is:

Limited to times when the employees of the primary employer are working on the premises.

Limited to times when the primary employer is carrying on his normal business there.

Confined to places reasonably close to where the employees of the primary employer are working.

Conducted so that the picket signs and the conduct of the pickets indicate clearly that the dispute is with the primary employer and not with the secondary employer.

These guidelines are known as the *Moore Dry Dock* standards, from the case in which they were first formulated by the NLRB. However, the NLRB has held that picketing at a common situs may be unlawful notwithstanding compliance with the *Moore Dry Dock* standards if a union's statements or actions otherwise indicate that the picketing has an unlawful objective.

In some situations a company may set aside a certain plant gate or other entrance to its premises for the exclusive use of a contractor. If a union has a labor dispute with the company and pickets the company's premises, including the gate so reserved, the union may be held to have violated Section 8(b)(4)(B). The Supreme Court has stated the circumstances under which such a violation may be found: "There must be a separate gate, marked and set apart from other gates; the work done by the men who use the gate must be unrelated to the normal operations of the employer, and the work must be of a kind that would not, if done when the plant were engaged in its regular operations, necessitate curtailing those operations."

However, if the reserved gate is used by employees of both the company and the contractor, the picketing would be considered primary and not a violation of Section 8(b)(4)(B).

Here is an important secondary-boycott case you should know about. The NLRB has held that a union which is striking a manufacturer may legally picket an independently owned and operated warehouse where some of the manufacturer's product is stored even if none of the manufacturer's employees works at the warehouse or ever goes near the place.

The union struck Cypress Gardens Citrus Products, which produced citrus-fruit concentrate. The company stored this product in a public warehouse owned by a neutral company. No Cypress employees worked in this warehouse. During the strike no Cypress trucks made deliveries to the warehouse. Common carriers received the product at the warehouse when sales were made. The union not only picketed truck loading docks but also a railroad siding.

The pickets carried signs reading: "Employees of Cypress Gardens Products are on strike. We have no dispute with any other employer." But the hard fact was that not only was Cypress barred from taking its product out of the warehouse but nineteen other employers, whose goods occupied 95 percent of the space in the warehouse, were likewise stymied.

The Board held that this picketing was not barred by the Labor Act. It said that Cypress was "present" in the warehouse because it could control the goods stored there. So the warehouse was a common situs and the picketing was primary, not secondary (*Auburndale Freezer Corp.*, 177 NLRB No. 108).

But the Fifth Circuit reversed and sent the case back to the Board with orders that the Board tell the union to cut out that kind of monkey business. The court pointed out that there was no strike against the Auburndale warehouse or any of the nineteen other employers who stored their products there. The processing plant operated by Cypress was the only situs involved in the dispute and thus the only place that could be lawfully picketed. The object of the picketing was to halt the operations of Auburndale and other employers who were total strangers to the whole controversy (*Auburndale Freezer Corp.* v. *NLRB*, 437 F.2d 1219, 75 LRRM 2752; review denied by Supreme Court, *United Steelworkers* v. *Auburndale Freezer Corp.*, 77 LRRM 2386).

In January 1971 the Supreme Court ruled on another important secondary-boycott case. In this case A, the primary employer, was doing some work as a subcontractor on a construction job. The work required the use of an electric welding machine. Members of the Iron Workers Union were doing the welding. The Operating Engineers wanted A to assign to their members the job of pushing the button which started the machine. They picketed B, the general contractor, to force it "to use its influence with" A to have the featherbedding job assigned to their members. The Supreme Court held that "to use its influence with" meant "to cease doing business with" and thus that the Operating Engineers had violated Section 8(b)(4)(B) (*NLRB* v. *Local 825, Operating Engineers; Burns & Roe, Inc.*, 76 LRRM 2129).

How to win. The moment the union starts to picket the secondary employer the primary employer should hasten to the NLRB's regional office and ask the regional director to seek an injunction in the federal district court. Subsection (1) of Section 10 says that whenever a company goes to the office of the Board's Regional Director and charges that a union is violating Section 8(b)(4)(B) the Regional Director shall drop everything else he may be doing and forthwith make an investigation. If after such investigation he has reasonable cause to believe the charge is true, he must petition the federal district court for injunctive relief pending the final adjudication of the Board as to whether or not 8(b)(4)(B) has been violated.

And if the boycott causes him any injury to his business, the secondary employer may sue the union for damages under Section 303 of the Act.

14

THE LAW OF THE
COLLECTIVE-BARGAINING GAME

COLLECTIVE BARGAINING IS defined in the Act in broad terms. Section 8(d), which was added in 1947, requires that an employer and the representative of his employees meet at reasonable times; that they confer in good faith about wages, hours, and other terms or conditions of employment for the purpose of negotiating an agreement and settling any question arising under the agreement; and that, upon the request of either party, the agreement be put in writing. As noted, these obligations are imposed equally on the employer and the representative of his employees; it is an unfair labor practice for either party to refuse to bargain collectively with the other. The obligation does not, however, compel either party to agree to a proposal by the other or to make a concession to the other.

The law developed by the Board and the courts over the years with respect to collective bargaining falls into several fairly distinct categories. In most of the cases before it, the Board has dealt with one or more of the following basic areas:

The conditions that must be met before bargaining is required.

Bargaining procedures and the negotiators qualified to bargain.

The proper subjects for collective bargaining.

The types of employer conduct which are in derogation of the duty to bargain in good faith.

The nature and scope of the union's duty to bargain and the types of union conduct which are in derogation of such duty.

Extenuating circumstances which affect the employer's duty to bargain.

The relation of individual grievances to the collective-bargaining scheme.

The notice requirements of Section 8(d).

The following conditions must be met before an employer is obliged to bargain: the union must have requested the employer to bargain; the union must demonstrate that it represents a majority of employees in the proposed unit, i.e., certification by the Board on presentation of authorization cards signed by a majority of the employees in the proposed unit which must be appropriate.

When these conditions have been met, the company is obliged to meet with the union's representative at reasonable times (you will recall the case in which the trial examiner held a company guilty of failure to bargain in good faith because over a period of a year only ten bargaining sessions with the union were held due to the fact that the company's spokesman, a lawyer, was so busy attending to his other clients [see page 88]).

Employers and unions are required to designate representatives who have adequate authority to engage in the give-and-take of good-faith bargaining, to explore the issues, and to bind their principals to any agreements which may be reached in the negotiations.

Most important to good-faith bargaining under the Act, each party must have "an open mind and a sincere desire to reach an agreement." An unyielding attitude at the bargaining table may be found to be at odds with the good-faith bargaining requirements of the Act. In each case the question is whether the party's conduct in bargaining, viewed in its entirety, showed that he did not negotiate with a good-faith intention to reach agreement.

However, the obligation to bargain does not compel the parties to reach an agreement. Collective-bargaining negotiations sometimes end in a deadlock in which neither side will make further concessions and each insists in good faith that its position on disputed issues is final. What constitutes a true impasse depends upon the facts of each particular case.

The parties are required to bargain about wages, hours, and other terms and conditions of employment. "Terms and conditions of employment" include union security agreements and checkoff of union dues. These items are called mandatory subjects of bargaining.

Matters which are outside the scope of the terms "wages, hours, and other terms and conditions of employment," and which are not independently unlawful, are referred to as permissible or non-mandatory subjects of bargaining. The parties are free to discuss and agree on nonmandatory subjects, but are not permitted to insist upon or bargain to an impasse on such subjects. Thus insistence on a performance bond against a possible breach of the collective-bargaining contract has been held an unfair labor practice, since such a bond is not held to be a compulsory bargaining subject. A "strike ballot" which would require the union to poll its members before calling a strike or refusing a final offer cannot be insisted upon by an employer, because it deals only with the relations between the employees and their union. The Board has also considered nonmandatory the subject of whether an employer should contribute to an industry promotion fund.

Not every case involves an outright refusal to bargain. But the following acts have been held to be in derogation of an employer's duty to bargain and thus a violation of what we have called the fifth commandment—a violation of Section 8(a)(5):

Unilateral action with respect to wages, hours, or terms or conditions of employment.

Refusal to furnish information required for intelligent bargaining.

Bargaining with individuals or minority groups.

Refusal to furnish proof of financial inability to meet wage demands if that is pleaded.

Imposing a prerequisite to bargaining which would require the union to forgo rights it has under the law; for example, demanding that the union withdraw a pending unfair-labor-practice charge.

Bargaining with other than the authorized bargaining representative.

This last transgression may take many forms: individual solicitation of striking employees to return to work accompanied by threats or promises of benefits; appeals directly to employees or a local union to bypass a certified international union; invitations to employees to deal directly with the employer on any grievance rather than through their duly chosen representative; insistence by an employer on a contract clause requiring approval of any subsequent strike by a majority of the employees.

Acts held to be in derogation of the union's duty to bargain and thus a violation of Section 8(b)(3), the counterpart of 8(a)(5), include insistence on illegal contract clauses, for example, closed-shop or unlawful union-security provisions, a welfare or retirement fund under which benefits would accrue only to union members, or an illegal "hot cargo" clause (an agreement not to handle the goods of a third party). But if the contract clause sought is itself lawful, insistence on the clause will not constitute a refusal to bargain even if carried out to the point of impasse so long as it covers a mandatory subject of bargaining. However, if a union insists that it will not sign a contract unless it includes proposals relating to nonmandatory subjects of collective-bargaining—such as a "work jurisdiction" clause embracing work performed by employees of another employer, or the employer's posting a performance bond— the union violates Section 8(b)(3).

Violation of Section 8(d) "notice rules" also involve a violation of Section 8(a)(5) by companies and Section 8(b)(3) by unions.

Section 8(d), inserted into the Act in 1947, is intended primarily to provide a "cooling off" period before a strike or lockout in connection with the modification or termination of a collective-bargaining agreement. This section requires that a party to the contract desiring to modify or terminate it must: (1) notify the other party in writing at least sixty days in advance of its termination date; (2) offer to meet and confer with the other party to negotiate a new contract or one containing the proposed modifications; (3) notify the Federal Mediation and Conciliation Service and the appropriate state mediation agency within thirty days after the first notice to the other party; and (4) withhold strike or lockout action, continuing the existing contract in full force and effect, for sixty days after the first notice or until the expiration date of the contract, whichever occurs later.

Most of the cases involving these provisions have involved

strikes and contract modifications rather than lockouts. If a union strikes to enforce demands for working conditions which would require modification of an existing agreement or the negotiation of a new contract, it violates its statutory duty to bargain if it has not complied with the procedures set forth in Section 8(d). Furthermore, employees participating in such a strike may lose their job rights and may be replaced by the employer, and the union may lose its bargaining rights through loss of majority status.

It is important to note that only economic strikes connected with the modification or termination of contracts are subject to these provisions and that many strikes are not of this type. Strikes protesting unfair labor practices of the employer, or strikes by unions having no contract with the employer, or even strikes to enforce the terms of the existing contract do not come under Section 8(d).

Unions have been held guilty of an unlawful refusal to bargain where they have not conformed to the statutory requirement to follow up their sixty-day notice to the employer with a thirty-day notice to both federal and state mediation agencies.

The consequences of failing to conform to 8(d) to the minute were illustrated on page 89.

Too much emphasis cannot be put on the provision in 8(d) that the requirement of bargaining in good faith does not compel either party to agree to a proposal or make a concession.

In 1970 the Supreme Court held that the Board could not order a company to grant the union a checkoff clause even though the company had been found not to have bargained in good faith on the checkoff issue (*H. K. Porter Co.* v. *NLRB*, 397 U.S. 99, 73 LRRM 2561).

But what constitutes "bargaining in good faith"? The Supreme Court has said that while "the Act does not encourage a party to engage in fruitless marathon discussions at the expense of frank statement of his position," it does require "more than a willingness to enter upon a sterile discussion of union-management differences." The distinction is said to be that between "hard bargaining" and "surface bargaining"—a difficult line to draw.

The Board adopted a trial examiner's recommendation that a union complaint that a company was refusing to bargain in good faith should be dismissed in the following case.

The trial examiner said that the issue was: "Did the company negotiate with the union in bad faith and with the intention of avoiding reaching agreement or conditioning agreement upon the union's acceptance of terms and conditions which the company knew or should have known were unacceptable to any self-respecting union?"

The Company had submitted bargaining proposals for a new contract to replace the existing contract which it had assumed when it leased the plant. The major proposals were these:

Reduce wage rate.

Eliminate checkoff clause.

Insert disclaimer of all past practices of predecessor employer.

Insert new management-right clause to reserve the sole right to set production standards, quotas, and subcontract work.

Insert clause giving company unlimited right to hire or transfer non-union employees to do production work in order to gain knowledge for service and/or positions outside the unit.

Eliminate two paid holidays—reducing from eight days to six.

Provide for six seniority groups instead of plant-wide seniority.

Provide vacation pay to be calculated as a percentage of straight-time earnings during prior calendar year rather than percentage of gross yearly earnings.

Eliminate antidiscrimination clause.

Reduce number of job classifications drastically.

The union, among other proposals, wanted an increase in pensions and an hourly wage increase of 50 cents the first year, 20 cents the second year, and 20 cents the third year.

When it gave the union notice that it wished to negotiate a new contract, the company also gave notice that it desired to terminate the pension plan in accordance with the provisions of the then-existing contract. On the day the old contract expired, the company notified employees that henceforth they would work in accordance with the terms and conditions it had offered the union.

The company terminated operation of the plant during a six-month strike without bargaining. It produced its books at the hearing, showing a loss after taxes for the prior three years of $991,000.

The decision took 23 legal-size pages typed single space. The trial examiner gave the details of each of thirteen bargaining sessions (including concessions made by both parties) and discussed the precedents for determining whether bargaining had been "hard bargaining," which is legal, or "surface bargaining," which violates the Act.

In its brief the company admitted that it went into negotiations with certain aims and goals and after stating what it had intended to get in the negotiations, continued as follows: "In short, the company acted like an intelligent management, for any management that goes into negotiations not knowing where it intends to be at the end of negotiations is (1) not real management, and (2) generally denuded" (*Manitowac Company, Inc.*, 186 NLRB No. 145-M).

You can make a firm offer at the first bargaining session and stick to it adamantly, but you must avoid:

Abrupt and outright rejection of a union proposal.

Stalling by postponing meetings.

Sending a negotiator who is not authorized to bind the company.

Refusing to produce proof of a plea of inability to pay.

Forcing negotiations to an impasse on a nonmandatory subject of bargaining, e.g., a pre-strike vote.

Refusing to bargain on mandatory subjects (anything that can be construed as involving "wages, hours, and other terms and conditions of employment").

Changing employment benefits unilaterally while negotiating and prior to impasse.

Refusing to execute a written contract incorporating any agreement already reached.

When an impasse occurs during the negotiation of an initial contract or following the expiration date of the current contract, an employer may unilaterally put into effect wage increases or other benefits equal to but not exceeding his last offer to the union (*NLRB* v. *Crompton-Highland Mills*, 337 U.S. 217).

The word "impasse" is defined by Webster as "affording no escape" but in labor relations law it is considered to mean a visceral feeling that the fellow across the table is not going to budge from the position he has taken during several negotiations any more than you are going to budge from the position you have taken.

When an impasse is reached during the negotiation of a reopener, the company may not act unilaterally but must continue in effect all pre-existing contractual commitments for the contract term. If it does not, it violates Section 8(a)(5) (*Standard Oil Company*, 174 NLRB No. 33).

It is essential that when bargaining begins, the parties agree that tentative agreements can be freely withdrawn later in the negotiations. A circuit court has held that technical contract law does not govern collective bargaining. Therefore when a company, after tentatively agreeing to several noneconomic matters, later withdrew these agreements and the employees went out on strike, the strike was an unfair-labor-practice strike because it was in protest of the company's failure to bargain collectively (*San Antonio Machine & Supply Corp.* v. *NLRB*, 363 F.2d 633).

You should not forget that under Section 8(b)(3) unions are also required to bargain in good faith and likewise cannot act unilaterally with respect to terms and conditions of employment. An employer cannot deprive an employee of his job by unilaterally deciding to contract out work. The question is: Can a union deprive an employer of production by unilaterally prescribing the amount of work an employee may perform? Thus, if a carpenter has been laying seven and one-half squares of wooden shingles in eight hours, may the union decide that in the future he may lay only six squares in eight hours?

"No," the Ninth Circuit Court told the National Labor Relations Board in a landmark decision. Such a unilateral decision changes the terms and conditions of employment and is a violation of the *Fibreboard* doctrine.

In the *Fibreboard* case, the Supreme Court held that an employer violated the duty to bargain in good faith imposed by Sections 8(a)(5) and 8(d) of Taft-Hartley when he unilaterally decided to substitute an independent contractor to perform the same work which employees had been doing (*Fibreboard Paper Products Corp.* v. *NLRB*, 379 U.S. 203).

But Section 8(a)(5), the court noted, has its counterpart in Section 8(b)(3), which together with Section 8(d) imposes on unions the duty to bargain in good faith concerning wages, hours, and other terms and conditions of employment.

There were no production limits fixed in the contract between the company and the union. A subsequent union rule limiting the number of shingles which might be laid by an employee was clearly a term and condition of employment. The rule had direct impact upon the employer, since it fixed the terms under which he procured the services of his employees.

So, concluded the court, such a rule could not be adopted until the union bargained with the employer to the point of impasse (*Associated Home Builders* v. *NLRB* F.2d 745).

15

HOW TO AVOID BARGAINING ABOUT
YOUR BUSINESS DECISIONS

IN 1964 THE SUPREME COURT held that a company was required to bargain concerning its decision to contract out maintenance work to a unionized independent contractor. The company employees doing the work had been terminated.

Chief Justice Warren, for the majority, held that contracting out must be considered "a term of employment." Justice Potter Stewart, in a concurring opinion, said:

> The Court most assuredly does not decide that every managerial decision which necessarily terminates an individual's employment is subject to the duty to bargain. Nor does the Court decide that subcontracting decisions are as a general matter subject to that duty. The Court holds no more than that this employer's decision to subcontract this work, involving the replacement of employees in the existing bargaining unit with those of an independent contractor to do the same work under similar conditions of employment, is subject to the duty to bargain collectively. [*Fibreboard Paper Products Corp.* v. *NLRB*, 379 U.S. 203]

Thereafter the apparent scope of the decision, which at first blush seemed to require bargaining about all management decisions which could conceivably involve terms and conditions of employment, was limited by the Board, although some decisions requiring "decision bargaining" are still asinine. For example:

A milk company was ordered to bargain about its decision to subcontract the distribution end of its business. But the Eighth Circuit refused to enforce the order, saying:

> Contrary to the situation in *Fibreboard*, then, there is more involved in *Adams Dairy* than just the substitution of one set of employees for

another. In *Adams Dairy* there is a change in basic operating procedure in that the dairy liquidated that part of its business handling distribution of milk products. Unlike the situation in *Fibreboard,* there was a change in the capital structure of *Adams Dairy.* . . . To require *Adams* to bargain about its decision to close out the distribution end of its business would significantly abridge its freedom to manage its own affairs [*NLRB* v. *Adams Dairy, Inc.,* 350 F.2d 108].

In another case, the company was required to bargain about increasing the price of a cup of coffee by one cent in its employees' cafeteria (*Westinghouse Electric Corp.,* 156 NLRB No. 96). The two dissenting members out of five said:

Collective bargaining is healthy, but if bargaining over a penny-a-cup increase in coffee becomes mandatory to the menu on the bargaining table, the result is liable to be acute indigestion . . . If this position is sustained, will the next step require bargaining over color of restroom walls, adequacy of pool table equipment, and the like? Penny-a-cup increases in carryout coffee are better left to the mercies of the voluntary action of the marketplace. When the cash register stops ringing, the price of coffee will begin descending.

A circuit court enforced the Board's order that the increase be rescinded and then be subjected to bargaining. But a dissenting judge had this to say:

We are reminded by the company of situations and conditions which may indirectly affect the interests of employees [and so be mandatory subjects of bargaining]. Bargaining representatives may argue that salaries of company officials are so high as to leave too little of company income for employees, that increases in the prices of company products will result in curtailed sales and less work for employees, that the company is spending too much or too little on research and development and is thereby jeopardizing future work opportunities or employee income, or that the company is manufacturing products to be used in a war or shipped to a nation of which the union disapproves . . . The Board, in this case, appears to follow its theory, as earlier articulated, that there's a duty imposed by Congress upon employers to bargain with their employees' representatives with respect to any matter which might in the

126

future emerge as a bone of contention between them, provided, of course, it should be a matter in respect to rates of pay, wages, hours or other conditions of employment . . . The statutory purpose may best be served by formulating, adopting, and applying a reasonable concept of "conditions of employment" in determining subjects of mandatory bargaining.

An employer must also bargain with the union if he wants to drop a product line and this action would be accompanied by layoffs, unless the union contract permits the elimination of products and the layoff of employees no longer needed (*Ador Corporation*, 150 NLRB No. 161); to raise the rent of company-owned houses rented by employees (*American Smelting & Refining Co.*, 167 NLRB No. 26); to consolidate operations through technological innovations (*Renton News Record*, 136 NLRB No. 1294); or to close one plant of a multiplant enterprise (*Ozark Trailers*, 161 NLRB No. 48).

A company need *not* bargain about its decision to sell part of its business (*General Motors Corp.*, 191 NLRB No. 149); contract out work if in the prior contract negotiations the union had failed to impose any restrictions on contracting out and there were thousands of subcontracts. In handing down this latter decision, the Board bore in mind particularly that the recurrent contracting out of work here in question was motivated solely by economic considerations; that it comported with the traditional methods by which the Respondent conducted its business operations; that it did not during the period in question vary significantly in kind or degree from what had been customary under past established practice; that it had no demonstrable adverse impact on employees in the unit; and that the Union had the opportunity to bargain about changes in existing subcontracting practices at general negotiating meetings [*Westinghouse Electric Corp.*, 150 NLRB No. 1547].

Nor must a company submit to bargaining if it contracts out work where it has a broad management-rights clause in the contract reserving this right (*General Motors Corp.*, 149 NLRB No. 40); if it goes out of business entirely (*Textile Workers* v. *Darlington Manufacturing Co.*, 380 U.S. 263); if it contracts out work that is not bargaining-unit work; or if it contracts out bargaining-unit work where the union in the past has unsuccessfully negotiated to limit the practice.

But note this one: The Board has held that an employer is under no duty to bargain about a decision to subcontract work because of a strike. The Teamsters Union had struck a warehouse. Its members normally delivered goods to A&P stores. The warehouse contracted with a trucking company to deliver the goods. The union told the stores that it intended to picket the warehouse trucks when they made deliveries and appeal to customers not to patronize the stores.

The Board held that the subcontracting was proper because (1) it was of a stopgap or temporary nature, necessary if the company was to continue its business relations with its customers; (2) the company continued to recognize the union as bargaining agent; (3) it offered to meet and bargain with the union concerning the subcontract in question; and (4) no jobs were eliminated because of the subcontract (*Empire Terminal Warehouse Co.*, 151 NLRB No. 125).

How to win. Although it often is impractical to call in a union to negotiate about a decision when it is essential that the decision be kept confidential, if that is not necessary, the thing to do is to give the union notice, tell it to come in to present any alternatives it may have that might cause you to change your tentative decision (like taking a pay cut!), and then when impasse has been reached, make the decision. The NLRB in apologizing for some of the absurdities brought about by the *Fibreboard* decision has just about suggested this. It has stressed that the Labor Act does not require a party bargaining about a mandatory subject of bargaining to make a concession.

Try to get a waiver clause into the contract like this one: "The corporation and the union, for the life of this agreement, each voluntarily and unqualifiedly waives the right, and each agrees that the other shall not be obligated to bargain collectively with respect to any subject or matter not specifically referred to or covered in this agreement."

Or try to get as broad a management-rights clause as possible. The Board has held that the following management-rights clause allows subcontracting of work without pre-decision negotiation if there is no loss of jobs:

The right to hire, promote, discharge or discipline for cause, and to maintain discipline and efficiency of employees, is the sole responsibility of the corporation except that union members shall not be discriminated against as such. In addition, the products to be manufactured, the location of the plants, the schedules of production, the methods, processes and means of manufacturing are solely and exclusively the responsibility of the corporation [*General Motors Corporation*, 149 NLRB No. 396].

16

MANAGEMENT VS. STRIKERS

STRIKES ARE EITHER economic strikes, unfair-labor-practice strikes, or illegal strikes.

An economic strike is one in which employees exert economic pressure on their employer in the hope of attaining their contract demands, whether a wage increase, a change in work rules, or a union shop.

An unfair-labor-practice strike is one in which employees protest an unfair labor practice committed by the employer. Perhaps the employer discharged a union steward without just cause, since his real reason for the discharge was that the steward vigorously enforced the employees' contract rights covering grievance procedures. But note that an economic strike may be held to have turned into an unfair-labor-practice strike if the employer commits an unfair labor practice which tends to prolong the strike; for example, if he refuses to reinstate the economic strikers when they unconditionally request reinstatement.

An illegal strike is one in violation of the Labor Act, such as a strike in violation of a "no strike" clause in the contract, or a strike to obtain economic benefits begun before the sixty-day notice period has run as required by the Act, or a strike in violation of the secondary-boycott ban in the Act.

Note that there is no need for a union to be in the picture when employees strike. When employees walk off the job in protest of such things as wages, unsafe or uncomfortable working conditions, or discriminatory hiring or promotion policies, they are engaged in "concerted activity" and they cannot be discharged or disciplined. To do so would violate the Labor Act.

Some strikes occur without warning. But most strikes are predictable. The grapevine, employee attitudes, or the union's posture at the bargaining table will tip you off. When indication of a strike appears, it is time to do some serious thinking. Can you take one? Or must you take one? Strikes are expensive. But giving away your shirt at the bargaining table may be even more expensive. You have to make up your mind. If you try to bluff and at the last moment the union calls your bluff, you're in for a rough future. The union thereafter will threaten to strike or even engage in a short strike when future contracts must be negotiated, and you will be over a barrel. You may be ruined. Make a firm decision. Either settle for the best terms you can get or draw a line in advance and swear, "Thus far and not an inch farther."

Before making this vital decision whether to take or not to take a strike, consider these points:

How long can you hold out?

What effect will your inability to operate have on your present or future business?

What about contractual commitments?

How many employees will honor the picket line?

How long can the union pay strike benefits, if any?

How easily can strikers obtain other employment?

Is unemployment compensation paid to strikers in your state?

Will banks, stores, auto dealers, etc., grant the strikers moratoria on mortgage and time payments?

Can you recruit replacements?

Has the union filed both the sixty-day notice on the company and the thirty-day notice on the Federal Mediation and Conciliation Service as required by Section 8(d) (see page 86)? If not, the strike is illegal and employees cease to be "employees" protected by the Act. They can be fired.

Are you ready to meet violence if you decide to keep the plant running?

What will community reaction be to the strike?

Is a short strike needed in any case, so everyone can blow off steam?

Do you have a nervous system that can take it if the strike drags on and the going gets rough?

If you decide that you are going to take a strike rather than give in to the union's demands, the very first thing you had better do is retain a labor relations lawyer. Not just a lawyer. There's been many a case where the company lawyer led the company into deep financial trouble. Get a labor relations lawyer. Labor relations law is a technical field. It is also a very dynamic, constantly changing set of rules. Something you do one day which is perfectly legal may be illegal six months later when the National Labor Relations Board considers the matter. And back pay to employees who have not been working can bankrupt a small company.

After you've hired a labor relations lawyer, consider drafting a pre-strike letter to the employees. Be careful not to suggest that if the employee doesn't report to work he will be deemed to have quit. Don't say strikers will be discharged. And although you have the right to replace economic strikers, be very sure you haven't committed an unfair labor practice within the last six months before you even threaten to seek replacements.

Send such a letter to the employee's home (wives don't like strikes!). Outline the company's last offer. Then you might add something like the following, which was approved by the NLRB in *F. W. Woolworth Co.* (111 NLRB No. 766):

Don't you know that the union positively cannot force or compel any company to give fantastic or crazy increases in wages? What they can do is to take the employees out on strike to attempt to force the company to give crazy increases. You might as well know it now—we will take a strike before we give any fantastic increases in wages.

We have taken strikes before. In New Albany, Indiana, for several months and in Port Arthur, Texas, since November 14, 1953—and that strike is still on.

Strikes hurt everybody but the union. The company loses sales and the employees lose wages.

Another thing, a striker might very well lose his job in an economic strike because the company can go right out and permanently hire an outsider and give that person the job of the striker. That is the law.

But watch that last paragraph. It may well be that if you have committed an unfair labor practice during the six months prior to the strike—like giving a noncustomary wage increase without consulting the union—a trial examiner may hold that the paragraph threatens unfair-labor-practice strikers with replacement and is thus in itself an unfair labor practice. For although economic strikers may be replaced permanently, unfair-labor-practice strikers may not be. When they make an unconditional request for reinstatement they must be given back their jobs even if this means you have to let replacements go to whom you have promised permanent jobs.

There are nearly always two strikes against the employer in a management-union contest!

Should you operate during the strike? This is a very tough decision to make. It must be made as long before the strike begins as possible. Of course, if your business is a public utility there is little choice if the service or product provided is essential to the health and welfare of the community. A business under severe delivery and performance demands from its customers is, for all practical purposes, in the same situation.

There is little point in trying to continue operations unless many of the employees do not support the strike and are willing to cross the picket line or there are sufficient prospective employees in the community who are willing to go through the picket line and replace the strikers. The union will try to stop passage through the picket line, and if it is militant, violence is a distinct possibility. Are adequate law-enforcement officers available to prevent violence so that nonstrikers and replacements can come to work? Are they willing to enforce the law?

If the attempt to continue operations fails, the strikers' morale gets a big boost. If it succeeds, however, chances are that the company will be able to bring the strike to an early end on acceptable terms.

It's a tough decision. If you do decide that you are going to try to operate during a strike, here is a list of things to do before the strike starts:

Notify customers and suppliers and hire warehouses to receive supplies on the day the strike begins.

Notify all law-enforcement authorities.

Notify the fire department of any special problems which might arise if fire should break out during the strike.

Set up a strike headquarters equipped with normal office machines and maintaining lists of names, addresses, and telephone numbers of all employees, customers and suppliers, law-enforcement officers, ambulance service, hospitals and doctors, etc.

Pick one executive as the only member of management who is to communicate with the news media.

Set up an information-gathering organization at strike headquarters. Some duties of this group: investigate all incidents connected with the strike and file written reports, maintain a strike log, photograph all strike incidents, keep a scrapbook of all newspaper clippings concerning the strike, make tape recordings of radio and television broadcasts concerning the strike.

Designate a separate gate for use of nonstriking employees exclusively.

Designate a separate gate for exclusive use by employees of independent contractors working on the premises.

Check security carefully, especially gates and fences, lighting of fences and parking lot, flammable goods, automatic sprinkler system, fire extinguishers, low roofs, power sources.

Review maintenance problems.

Don't make any agreement with the union concerning entry to company property during the strike, such as allowing employees to come into the plant "to pick up their tool boxes."

Don't agree that the last paycheck will be mailed out "at the usual time." Send them out at once, not only so that they will be spent as soon as possible but also to be certain you don't violate any state laws requiring that wages be paid within a certain period after the work has been done.

Supervisory communication. Tell supervisors not to visit strikers at their homes. The NLRB may claim you were trying to negotiate directly with the employee through the foreman and thus were trying to undermine the union.

But if a supervisor is approached by a striker, the supervisor may:

Tell him that the law permits the employer to hire a replacement for anyone who engages in an economic strike.

Remind him of what benefits he has at present (but the supervisor must not intimate anything about benefits in the future or make threats about the future).

Remind him about the disadvantages of being on strike—loss of income, the requirement to serve on the picket line, etc.

Tell him that throughout the negotiations the company felt, and continues to feel, that its proposals are fair.

WARNING: Tell supervisors not to threaten any employee or promise him any benefit, and not to disparage the union. They should also be warned to make no comment whatsoever to the media.

Replacing economic strikers. Although you cannot fire an employee because he engages in an economic strike, you have the right to replace him. You can offer such a replacement a permanent job, and you do not have to restore the striker to his job so long as the replacement doesn't depart.

But if after the employee has made an unconditional offer to return to work, either individually or through the union, you discharge the replacement or he quits, you must seek out the striker and offer him reinstatement unless he has obtained another permanent job or unless you can show that there is a legitimate and substantial reason for not doing so; for example, that he was guilty of extreme misconduct during the strike.

This is one reason why you should endeavor to collect evidence of all picket-line misconduct during the strike, including photographs, affidavits of witnesses, etc. Assign one or more supervisors the duty of observing and filing a written daily report of all incidents both inside and outside the plant.

The persons so designated should include in the daily report:

136

The time the picket line was established, discontinued, or resumed, as the case may be.

The number of pickets, significant changes in numbers, names and jobs of pickets, if possible, and other relevant information about the picket line.

Specific description of picket-line conditions.

The presence or absence of union officers, business agents and international representatives or other nonemployees. The presence or absence of signs, weapons, barricades, and other such paraphernalia.

Names of employees going through the picket line.

A record of all incident reports, photographs, affidavits and statements of witnesses obtained during the day.

Miscellaneous information relevant to the company's evaluation of strike conduct.

Examples of incidents that should be promptly investigated and reported: threatening phone calls received by workers who have crossed the picket line; damage to company property or the property of employees; throwing of objects at employees or company property; violence, rioting, or assault by strikers and pickets; other acts of intimidation.

The significance of detailed and accurate reports cannot be overemphasized. They are especially important in connection with future legal action—defending against unjustified unemployment-compensation claims, criminal prosecutions, damage suits, and arbitration that might result from the strike settlement.

You must not offer replacements "superseniority," i.e., place their names on top of the seniority list to guarantee them against layoff if business slumps after the strike is over. Nor may you pay them higher rates than were made in your last offer to the union before the strike was called. The same rule holds for employees who did not go out on strike and who crossed the picket line to work.

Your obligation to bargain. When a strike occurs after an impasse has been reached, the strike itself breaks the impasse. Accordingly, you must not refuse to bargain with the union during the strike. This obligation does not exist, however, if the strike is illegal, such as one in breach of a "no strike" clause. Only when the union terminates such an illegal strike does the obligation to bargain renew itself. But in such a case be sure to reserve the right to discipline employees for illegal actions during the strike.

If a strike occurs while a contractor is working at the plant, you may set up a "reserved gate" for the contractor and if the union pickets that gate it can be enjoined by a federal district court. For this purpose you construct or set aside a separate gate; put up a sign saying that this particular gate may be used solely by employees of the contractor; enforce the rule on the sign vigorously—don't permit employees who haven't struck to use it to enter or leave the plant.

Note that a "reserved gate" is valid only if the work being done by the contractor is not related to the normal operations of the company, i.e., it must be of a kind that would not, if performed when the plant was engaged in its regular operations, necessitate the curtailing of those operations.

Beware of converting an economic strike into an unfair-labor-practice strike. If the NLRB finds that during a strike a company committed an unfair labor practice that prolonged the strike, it will hold that the strike was "converted" into an unfair-labor-practice strike. This means that when the strikers make an unconditional offer to return to work, they must be reinstated and "permanent" replacements hired after the date of the unfair labor practice must be let go. Back pay runs from the date of the unconditional offer to return to work until date of reinstatement.

This "conversion" doctrine often comes into play when, in warning economic strikers that they will be replaced, an employer includes in his letter a threat of discharge if they don't return. The context of the following letter has been approved by the Board.

In good faith, we have tried for more than three weeks to provide a safe and dignified way for production workers as a group to return to work, so that your regular paychecks and our production can continue while a new contract is being negotiated.

138

Now we must ask you to make your decision on this matter, because it is our duty to restore the company to full production without further delay. If you do not return to work by Friday, June 8, we will be compelled to fill your job with a permanent replacement.

We can give assurance that your job status will be protected only until 5 P.M. on Friday, June 8.

Illegal strikes. If employees engage in an illegal strike they can be fired and the union can be sued for damages. Illegal strikes include sit-down strikes; strikes in violation of the labor contract, e.g., in violation of a "no strike" clause; strikes in violation of the Labor Act; a strike by a minority of union members to force the hand of the union's negotiators; a strike in protest against an unfair labor practice where the employees do not take reasonable precautions to protect the plant from imminent foreseeable damage, e.g., if they leave supplies or equipment in such a condition that they be damaged.

Until June, 1970 about all an employer could do when employees struck in violation of a "no strike" clause in their contract was to sue the union for damages and fire the employees. The first alternative is not very satisfactory for reasons too complicated to explain, and as for the second, only a fool will fire his whole work force. Thus the only weapon worth much was to fire the ringleaders of the illegal strike. But in June 1970, after taking the opposite view for many years, the Supreme Court in *Boys Markets, Inc.* v. *Retail Clerks* (398 U.S. 235) held that an employer can get an injunction in a federal district court if:

(1) The district judge finds that both the company and the union are contractually bound to arbitrate the grievance which caused the strike.

(2) The judge orders the company to arbitrate as a condition of obtaining an injunction against the strike.

(3) The judge finds that violations of the no-strike clause are occurring and will continue, or have been threatened and will be committed.

(4) The judge finds the violations of contract have caused or will cause irreparable injury to the company.

(5) The judge finds the company will suffer more from the denial of an injunction than will the union from its issuance.

The first three "ifs" are easy. As to the fourth and fifth, the facts in the case before the Supreme Court illustrate them:

The company operated a supermarket. Its frozen-foods supervisor and certain members of his crew who were not members of the bargaining unit began to rearrange the frozen food in the showcases. The union demanded that the company require bargaining-unit members to take the food out of the cases, carry it to the main freezer located in the back room of the supermarket, and then carry it back and rearrange it as the supervisor had done.

When the company refused to accede to this demand a strike was called. The union began to picket. The company sent a telegram to the union demanding that the dispute be submitted to arbitration and that the union stop the strike.

The contract contained a broad arbitration clause covering "any and all disputes" and requiring arbitration on written demand of either party.

The court approved the finding of the district court judge that "serious loss of business patronage" would mean "irreparable injury" to the employer and that thus "greater injury will be inflicted upon [the employer] by the denial of relief than will be inflicted upon [the union] by the issuance of such relief."

Beware you don't condone illegal conduct. "Condonation" is the doctrine that you cannot forgive a sin and then punish the sinner. If an employer, following a strike in violation of a "no strike" clause (an unprotected activity), condones that unprotected activity by reinstating employees, he cannot later plead that unprotected activity as justification for reprisals subsequently visited on the employees. Here's an example of condonation:

The company discharged an employee named Christiansen when he refused to accept a temporary assignment to another job. Mason, a union steward, who was working nearby, said: "Come on fellows, we're walking out until he comes back to work." Eight of the approximately twenty-eight employees left the plant at 10:30 A.M. that day, admittedly in violation of a no-strike provision in their contract.

None of the employees who walked off the job returned to work that day. At 2 P.M., Bates, the company's manager, went outside and told the strikers that they could return to work but that Christiansen was fired.

The next day all the employees who had walked off the job, including Mason, worked all day. Nothing was said by any supervisor about the walkout. Late that afternoon Mason was discharged because he had instigated the strike.

The Board ordered Mason's reinstatement with back pay (*Packers Hide Association, Inc.*, 152 NLRB No. 167).

How to win. In a situation like this, a company should brand the strike as a breach of contract and state that all the strikers are to be disciplined. It should emphasize that returning to work will not cause it to "forgive and forget" or mitigate discipline to be meted out to those who led as well as those who participated.

Arbitrator Harry J. Dworkin of Cleveland has pointed out a more subtle but equally damaging form of condonation: discharge accompanied by an offer to rehire as a new employee. In this case most of the company's employees either failed to enter the plant or called in sick. The activity was clearly in violation of a contract clause banning strikes or slowdown. The same clause read that "any violation of this provision may be made the subject of disciplinary action, including discharge." The strike was not sanctioned by the union, whose officers, in fact, used their best efforts to stop it.

The company discharged all the participants by letter. But the letter contained the following sentence: "Should you desire to apply for reemployment your application will be given our consideration."

The arbitrator found that the strikers had violated the no-strike clause and could have been properly discharged. But he went on to hold that the notice of discharge coupled with the proposal to reemploy the strikers as new hirees was a punitive measure at variance with established disciplinary concepts.

He ordered reinstatement without loss of seniority but without back pay, saying:

In the judgment of the arbitrator the decision to discharge for just cause contemplates that the employee is beyond rehabilitation and/or corrective discipline; that he has committed a breach of his obligations of sufficient seriousness to require forfeiture of his right to continued employment and benefits. It appears to the arbitrator that where discharge is accompanied by an offer to re-hire as a new employee, this is, in fact, a form of discipline other than discharge. The disciplinary penalty, i.e., discharge coupled with an offer to re-hire as a new employee, when considered together with its implications is in substance a penalty in the form of forfeiture of seniority, vacation benefits accruing by reason of length of service, preferential consideration in the event of promotion or layoffs, preferential right to perform available overtime, shift preferences and extinction of other benefits that accrue under the contract by reason of length of service. The contract does not contemplate loss of seniority and related benefits as a proper form of corrective discipline. The arbitrator feels that there is both reason and contractual support for the union's statement that, "when it hired the same people with no showing in change of attitude on the part of those it re-hired, the company pointed up its own contradictory position."

The arbitrator finds logic in the union's reasoning, and inquiry: "How then does the company explain its re-hiring of those it had already found to be incorrigible?" The issuance of a discharge penalty coupled with an offer of reemployment as a new hiree is inconsistent with the concept of corrective discipline as it exists in the context of industrial relations; the procedure utilized by the company was intended to retain a number of the work force who had participated in the illegal work stoppage, coupled with a form of punishment that was contractually unauthorized, and improper.

The employer should send this memo to all supervisors outlining what they should do when the boys walk off the job in violation of a "no strike" clause in the contract.

Stay on the job. Don't run to the office. Note everything that happens. Notify the personnel officer (so he may notify the union officers).

Tell the guys, "Listen, you fellows, this stoppage is a violation of the labor contract. Get back on the job and let's handle your beef as a grievance."

Learn who the leaders are.

Note whether stewards or other union officials participate.

Don't negotiate with anyone.

Write a detailed memo about what happened.

Misconduct of strikers during a lawful strike. Strikers who engage in serious misconduct in the course of a strike may be refused reinstatement in their former jobs. This applies to both economic strikers and unfair-labor-practice strikers. Serious misconduct has been held to include violence, threats of violence, and similar misconduct. The Supreme Court has ruled that a "sit-down" strike, in which employees simply stay in the plant and refuse to work, thus depriving the owner of his property, is not protected by the law. Where an unfair labor practice by the employer provokes an unfair-labor-practice strike, this fact may be considered in the determination of whether misconduct by strikers will bar their reinstatement. Examples of serious misconduct that could cause the strikers to lose their right to reinstatement are: physically blocking persons from entering or leaving a struck plant; threatening violence against nonstriking employees entering a plant; and attacking management representatives.

17

WHAT TO WATCH OUT FOR WHEN THE UNION CALLS OFF AN ECONOMIC STRIKE

UP UNTIL 1968, pursuant to the Supreme Court's 1938 decision in *NLRB* v. *Mackay Radio & Telegraph Co.* (304 U.S. 333), a strike against an employer not "guilty of [any] act denounced by the statute" was held to be an economic strike rather than an unfair-labor-practice strike, and the employer had the right to hire permanent replacements in order to keep his plant operating.

Then the NLRB changed the rules in *NLRB* v. *Laidlaw Corp.* (414 F.2d 99). These new rules were approved by a circuit court. The Supreme Court refused to review that court's decision.

Here are the new rules:

An employer commits an unfair labor practice when he terminates the employment status of *replaced economic strikers* after their unconditional offer to return to work and fails to offer them reinstatement upon the departure of their "permanent" replacements until he can prove a legitimate and substantial business reason for terminating them.

The employer has the duty to *seek out* such strikers and offer them reinstatement, since their unconditional request to return to work is a *continuing offer* which does not terminate merely because on the day it was made no job vacancies happened to be available.

The remedy for such violation of the Labor Act shall be reinstatement with pay running back to the date each striker's replacement departed without the striker having been offered reinstatement.

It is immaterial whether the employer's conduct was lawful at the time it was performed; labor lawyers and industrial relations directors must be good prophets or advise at their peril. Whether the striker's vested interest in his job or any substantially equivalent job is perpetual or whether it lapses after the passage of time must be left to future cases for determination. Likewise, the extent of the effort the employer must make to seek out the strikers and offer them reinstatement as permanent replacements depart must be left to future cases for determination.

These were the facts: the Pulp, Sulphite and Paper Mill Workers and the company were unable to agree on wages. The employees were on strike for a month. Then, in a group and on the same day, each employee gave the company notice that he unconditionally offered to return to work immediately. At that time all but five jobs had been filled by permanent replacements. The company reinstated five of the strikers.

After the mass offer to return unconditionally to work, individual strikers from time to time repeated their offer to return to work unconditionally. But from the beginning of the strike the company had adopted a fixed policy with reference to strikers who sought reinstatement: it gave reinstatement only to those striker-applicants who applied for reinstatement on the *very day* vacancies occurred due to the departure of permanent replacements. If there were no vacancies on the day of such applications, the company washed the applicants' names off its records and hired new employees.

When they came to realize this, some of the reinstated strikers walked out again and picketed with a sign changed to read: "Local 681 International Brotherhood of Pulp, Sulphite and Paper Mill Workers on Strike Protesting Unfair Labor Practices." The Board thought the company's behavior turned the economic strike into an unfair-labor-practice strike.

After the end of the strike the company continued to advertise for employees and indeed hired fifty new employees in the month following the strikers' mass offer to return to work.

The court gave short shrift to the company's arguments that:

(1) the Board's decision "creates in perpetuity a vested interest of the employee in the job, or any substantially equivalent jobs, he held when he first went on strike";

(2) the Board's decision was erroneous because it was based on its finding that the strikers' requests to return to work were *continuing in*

nature, whereas the strikers' requests for reinstatement read: "I am un-conditionally offering to return to work immediately"; "immediately" meant now, at this moment, not sometime in the future; there were only five vacancies at the time and they were filled "immediately" by reinstating five strikers;

(3) even if the Board's holding was correct, the imposition of back-pay liability was improper because the revised Board policy was being applied to conduct which was lawful at the time the conduct was performed.

Senior Circuit Judge Major filed a red-hot dissent. He said:

My mind rebels against imposing upon an employer a huge penalty for failure to anticipate what the Supreme Court might hold at some time in the future. Moreover, I doubt if this court has reviewed the record in a labor case where the employer under the advice of knowl-edgeable counsel so scrupulously adhered to the law as taught by the Board and the courts. . . .

Enforcement of the Board's order means from now on that an employer when faced with the problem of his rights and obligations in a labor dispute cannot safely rely on the advice of counsel, pronounce-ments of the Labor Board or court decisions for the law by which he should chart his course. Instead, he must be endowed with a power of prophecy sufficiently great to enable him to anticipate that the Board may change the law and make illegal that which was legal.

Laidlaw was a great labor victory. It means that management's favorite argument—made, by the way, by the Laidlaw manage-ment—that "you are free to strike, but we are free to hire a re-placement for you and if we do your job is lost forever," has been stripped of much of its punch. It means that union leaders now have a strong argument with which to urge economic strikers to "hang on." It also means longer strikes.

Laidlaw puts an additional burden on management. Employees furnish their names and telephone numbers on their employment applications, but it is common knowledge that this information is not kept current. Personnel officers henceforth should take steps to see that the information *is* kept current. One of these days the Board may well hold that if management doesn't possess the information by which it can notify a striker that a job is waiting for him, it must pay him retroactively to the date a notification bounces back stamped "Not at This Address."

Subsequent cases have fleshed out the bare bones of the *Laidlaw* doctrine to some extent. In one case the union made an unconditional application for reinstatement of eight employees who had been permanently replaced during an economic strike to win contract terms. The trial examiner stated the facts with respect to each of the eight. The decision is authority for the following subsidiary rules:

Which strikers have been replaced by persons hired during the strike may be determined by application of the seniority principle, that is, the person with the least seniority in a particular job classification or department may be considered to have been replaced by the first person hired in that job classification.

A striker who acquires a regular and substantially equivalent job with another employer *before* his replacement is hired ceases to be an employee of the struck firm and has no right to reinstatement when the replacement quits, even though he himself has left the new job.

A striker who acquires a regular and substantially equivalent job *after* his replacement is hired likewise ceases to be an employee of the struck firm.

When *any* job comes open which a replaced striker who *has not* lost his employee status could fill, not merely when the specific replacement leaves who was hired during the strike for his job, the striker is entitled to reinstatement.

A new job is a "substantially equivalent job" even though it is a different job from that which the striker performed for the struck employer and even though with *working overtime* his present income is "somewhat" smaller than his income when he worked for the struck employer.

The following facts do not constitute a "legitimate and substantial business reason" for not reinstating strikers after their replacements have departed: that the *Laidlaw* decision is wrong and should be reversed; that a striker by applying for work elsewhere has abandoned the employee relationship; that a striker has not complied with the employer's policy of hiring only at the plant door by failing to make applications at times when a job was available; that only a *part-time job* was available when a replacement departed; that a striker did not *personally* make an unconditional offer to return to work (the union's offer is sufficient); that a striker did not notify the employer when the striker changed his address; that a striker went into business for himself *after* his replacement departed; that a striker retained $11.73 belonging to the employer and did not return it until the employer asked for it (striker had collected from a cash customer after servicing an airplane during a night shift just before the strike began).

An employer satisfies his obligation under *Laidlaw* when he sends a letter to the employee's last known address when a job is available or *notifies the union that the job is available.*

The burden of seeking the strikers to offer reinstatement is on the employer; the striker need not seek out the employer so that an offer can be made to him (*Little Rock Airmotive, Inc.*, Case 26-CA-3319 [1970]).

In a second case a trial examiner's decision was handed down which covers a problem that often arises when a union calls it quits and requests the unconditional reinstatement of economic strikers. What if one of them returns to work and is found to be disabled? Does his right to reinstatement continue?

The striker came back to work August 5, and the company physician found he had a hernia. Thereupon the company scratched him off a preferential hiring list it had prepared.

The employee had the hernia fixed and on September 29 showed up with proof that he was able to work and reapplied for a job. The company refused his application and thereafter gave available jobs to others.

The General Counsel argued that the employee's right to reinstatement continued after August 5 for a "reasonable period" and that September 29 was within such reasonable period.

The company challenged this "vague theory." It asked questions like these: May a "reasonable period" extend for years? What medical problems would disqualify an employee for a job? What if the employee waited a year before consenting to the

149

hernia operation? What if the employee happened to be a Christian Scientist? How much medical knowledge is to be charged to an employer? etc.

The trial examiner ordered reinstatement with back pay. She agreed with the General Counsel's theory and held that the period involved was "reasonable" (*American Gypsum Co.,* Case No. 28-CA-1802 [1970]).

In a third case there was violence on the picket line during an economic strike which lasted longer than twelve months. The strikers were permanently replaced. After the strike ended, ten strikers made unconditional requests for reinstatement. Thereafter the company hired thirteen new employees to fill vacancies caused by the departure of permanent replacements.

The company defended its failure to reinstate by citing Section 9(c)(3) and contending that "an economic striker ceases to be an employee when he has engaged in an economic strike for more than twelve months' duration and during such period has been permanently replaced."

The trial examiner held that Section 9(c)(3), which covers voting rights of strikers, had *no relevance* with respect to determining the reinstatement rights of strikers. He also noted that in 1947, at the time of the Taft-Hartley changes in the Act, various amendments were proposed to Section 2(3) (which defines "employee") which, *on bases other than time,* would have brought about the termination of the "employee" status of economic strikers and that Congress rejected these proposals (*Hartmann Luggage Company,* Case 26-CA-3360 [1970]).

In a fourth case a trial examiner had held that the picket-line misconduct of eight women strikers furnished a legitimate and substantial business reason for not reinstating them. The Board, although agreeing with the trial examiner that their conduct was "improper and not to be condoned," ordered their reinstatement.

Here's some of what the she-devils did—what the Board called "relatively minor misconduct":

Pauline with some twenty-five other pickets prevented a truck from entering the company's plant for ten minutes until dispersed by the police; called Linda S. and others who were driving from the plant "sons of bitches"; hooted and jeered as the company president was leaving the plant and blocked the exit, slowing the car's departure; yelled at two women supervisors leaving the plant, "Why are you so late? Did you have to stay in there and .... old Cady before you could go home?" (Cady was plant manager); rushed at a woman employee, who had stopped to inspect the damage to her car from a rock thrown by another picket, and threatened to "get" her; rocked the car of another employee and broke the windshield.

Irene, Pauline's comrade in arms in the above activity, stood by and cheered while male employees beat up nonstriking employees; called another employee a "black S.O.B."; sent word to one male nonstriker via a salesman that she would beat the hell out of him when she got back to work.

Lorene told a male supervisor that it was a shame to have to kill him, as he was too young to die, on the day before he was beaten up and his car damaged by her fellow employees; she also scattered tacks in the plant's driveway to cause flat tires (*Hartmann Luggage Company,* 183 NLRB No. 128).

An unfair-labor-practice strike. Where one of the causes of a strike is conduct of a company which is an unfair labor practice— for example, unilaterally discontinuing a benefit, such as the payment of transportation expenses—the strike is an unfair-labor-practice strike and the striking employees are entitled to reinstatement upon their unconditional request to return to work, notwithstanding that they may have been replaced in the interim. The replacements must be let go. Moreover, if a company merely threatens to replace them it violates the Act (*United States Tube & Foundry Co.,* 188 NLRB No. 60).

18

PROTECTING YOUR EMPLOYEE
FROM HIS UNION'S WRATH

SINCE ANYONE CAN file a charge that a union has committed an unfair labor practice, a company may file a charge that a union has violated Section 8(b)(1)(A) of the Act. That section makes it an unfair labor practice for a union to coerce an employee who exercises his Section 7 right to refrain from concerted activities (i.e., from striking) but goes on to say that "this paragraph shall not impair the rights of a labor organization to prescribe its own rules with respect to the acquisition or retention of membership therein."

In 1967 the Supreme Court held that a union did not violate this section when it imposed a "reasonable" fine on a member and endeavored to collect it by court action because he had crossed an authorized picket line and gone to work (*NLRB* v. *Allis-Chalmers Manufacturing Co.*, 388 U.S. 175).

Thereafter many cases considered the question: What is a reasonable fine?

In 1970 the NLRB held that it has no authority to rule on the reasonableness of fines levied by a union on its members for going through a picket line and working during an authorized strike. A union can fine such a member in any amount (*International Association of Machinists* [Arrow Development Co.], 185 NLRB No. 22).

In a second case decided the same day, the Board held that a union may not fine employees who cross a picket line and work after they submit resignations to the union. The Board also held that employees may be fined (presumably in any amount) who do not submit their resignations until after they cross the picket line to go to work (*The Boeing Company,* 185 NLRB No. 23).

In the *Arrow Development* case there was a union-shop clause in the contract, which had expired when the strike began. The fine, according to the dissenting Board member, was "greater than the wages earned during the strike." This means that all the union has to do to stop its members from working during a strike is to announce that any member who does so will be fined in the amount he earns plus the cost of collecting the fine. For the union in this case got a court judgment for the fine plus costs and then attempted to collect on the judgment by garnisheeing the employee's wages.

In the *Boeing* case there was a maintenance-of-membership clause rather than a union-shop clause. That is, those who were members on the day the contract became effective had to maintain that membership to keep their jobs; newly hired employees did not have to join the union. The strike began after the contract expired.

The following cases illustrate various situations where a union may and may not fine a member or ex-member.

A trial examiner has held that an international union which violates a no-strike clause also violates the Labor Act when it fines members of a local who cross the picket line to go to work.

The contract between the International Chemical Workers and the Dow Chemical Company contained the following clauses:

It is agreed that there shall be no strikes, walkouts, lockouts or any other interruption of work during the period of this Agreement.

Work shall not be interrupted because of any disputes, disagreements between or with persons, corporations, unions, or associations which are not parties to this agreement provided that this section shall not be construed as to compel the members of the union to go through a picket line duly authorized by the International Chemical Workers Union, Akron, Ohio. There is no intent to compel employees to cross picket lines elsewhere.

Local 23 struck Dow at Pittsburg, California. Twelve days later a picket line sanctioned by the international union was set up by

Local 598 at Dow's Torrance, California, plant. Seven members of Local 598 crossed this picket line to work. Thereafter these members were fined for so doing and suspended from membership until they paid the fines. Dow filed a charge with the Board that thereby the international union had violated Section 8(b)(1)(A) of the Labor Act.

Interpreting the contract clause quoted above, the trial examiner held that it was a broad, unambiguous "no strike" clause modified only to the extent that if a dispute arose between Union X and Company Y, Dow could not compel its employees to cross a picket line set up by Union X even though that picket line had been authorized by the International Chemical Workers Union. To penalize members for refusing to participate in the violation of a "no strike" clause despite the proviso in 8(b)(1)(A), he concluded, would provide an incentive to unions and members to violate contracts (*Dow Chemical Company*, Case No. 31-CB-569 [1971]).

The NLRB has ruled that a union member can be expelled for filing a decertification petition with the Board but that he cannot be fined.

The Board held that the union violated the Labor Act when it imposed a $100 fine on an employee for circulating and filing a petition seeking to decertify the union as bargaining representative of the company's employees. It thought the right reserved to the union in the Labor Act "to prescribe its own rules with respect to the . . . retention of membership" did not apply.

The union must be able to protect itself from a fifth column—an attack from within. Expulsion achieves that end, but it does not deter a member from petitioning for decertification, since his job cannot be made to depend on union membership. But fining is not defensive; it is punitive—punishing for exercising a right granted by the Labor Act. (*Blackhawk Tanning Co*, 178 NLRB No. 25 [1969]).

A trial examiner has also held that a union violates Section 8(b)(1)(A) of the Act if it fines a member for seeking information from the Board about its decertification processes and calling a meeting of employees at which such information was disseminated (*George E. Clemence,* An Individual, Case 7-CB-2100 [1970]).

A trial examiner has held that a union was protected by the proviso to Section 8(b)(1)(A) of the Labor Act when it fined members for going to the company with a cock-and-bull story concerning a wildcat strike while the union was processing a grievance in an attempt to get their jobs back. The proviso guarantees to unions the right to prescribe their own rules with respect to retaining membership.

Thirteen employees in a single department of a plant walked off the job in violation of a "no strike"clause. The fourteenth, a union steward, went home half an hour ahead of them. But he had been excused, having falsely stated that his wife was ill.

The company promptly discharged the thirteen. They tried, without success, to persuade the union to strike the plant. The most the union would do for them was to file a grievance and agree to take it to arbitration. But the union warned them that the chance of winning was minimal and that, in any case, about three months would pass before an arbitrator's decision would be had.

The thirteen then went to the company and persuaded it that the shop steward had led them astray. This, the trial examiner later found, was a lie. The company reinstated them at the third step of the grievance procedure. It then fired the steward. An arbitrator upheld the discharge.

The union learned the truth. It fined the thirteen. All but one paid up. The union sued No. 13 in state court to collect the fine. Both No. 13 and the company (not knowing it had been bamboozled) charged the union with an unfair labor practice.

The trial examiner recommended dismissal of the complaint. He found that the thirteen, acting unilaterally and outside the contractually established grievance procedure, had gone directly to the company to further their individual interests against those of the union as an entity (*United Steelworkers of America,* Case 30-CB-253 [1969]).

Section 9(a) of the Labor Act reads in part: "Any individual or a group of employees shall have the right at any time to present grievances to their employer and to have such grievances adjusted, without the intervention of the bargaining representative, as long as the adjustment is not inconsistent with the terms of a collective-bargaining contract or agreement then in effect; provided further, that the bargaining representative has been given opportunity to be present at such adjustment."

However, it is one thing for a discharged employee to go to the employer himself to handle his own affairs. It is quite another for him to file a contractual grievance through his union and then during the heat of the proceeding insist that it be litigated as he, in disagreement with the union, sees fit, even going to the extent of simultaneously dealing with the company representative behind the union's back.

A trial examiner has held that a union violates the Labor Act when it tries and imposes punishment (a fine) on one who has mailed a resignation of membership to the union, even if the resignation was never received. "Although the United States mail is not an infallible institution, we are not persuaded that the presumption of delivery has been overcome in this case," said the trial examiner.

John J. Hurley was an employee of The Chesapeake and Potomac Telephone Company. The employees were represented by the Communications Workers of America, whose International president is the much respected Joseph A. Bierne.

Back in 1965 on one of those occasions when Negoes were burning and looting in Washington, D.C., to establish civil rights, Hurley's local was due to strike. Bierne called off the strike "for the good of the community and the country."

At a subsequent meeting of the local, Hurley, a former chief steward, reproached the local's vice-president because the "civil disturbance situation was one where the union had the company with its pants down" and "Bierne had no right to call it off." The vice-president stoutly asserted that he and the other officers of the local did not necessarily represent the wishes of the members but the policies of the international union.

"You've just lost yourself a member" was Hurley's angry reply, and he flounced out. The next day Hurley wrote a letter of resignation in the presence of a witness. In the presence of the same witness, he dropped in a mailbox an envelope addressed to the union containing the one-sentence message: "I resign from membership in Local 2108, Communications Workers of America."

With this terse message Hurley enclosed a check covering the equivalent of dues for the next three months. The check was cashed. The resignation was never seen again.

Thereafter the union struck. Hurley walked right through the picket line and no one moved to stop him. But he was tried in absentia and fined $500.

On September 3, 1965, Hurley filed a charge with the NLRB stating that in trying him when he was not a member the union had violated his Section 7 right to refrain from concerted activities.

The trial examiner held that trying and fining Hurley when he was not a member of the union did violate his Section 7 right to refrain from concerted activities. Since the check arrived, the resignation must have also, he said. Because there was proof of mailing, the trial examiner could have come to the same conclusion even if there had been no canceled check to show that the envelope containing the resignation must have arrived.

There is a presumption of delivery when an envelope is dropped into a U.S. mailbox: delivery "within two or three days" said the optimistic trial examiner (*John J. Hurley,* Case 5-CB-861 [1969]).

A trial examiner has held that a company committed an unfair labor practice when it insisted that, before it would sign a contract incorporating terms which had been agreed upon, the union must agree orally to withdraw substantial fines imposed on employees who had crossed a picket line to return to work. He further held that the company's demand instantly converted an economic strike into an unfair-labor-practice strike.

Note carefully that the company had not insisted that a clause to such effect be included in the new collective-bargaining agreement; it had merely asked the union to forget about collecting $500 fines from six women employees.

An economic strike had begun on May 14, 1968. During the

strike the six women crossed the picket line and returned to work. They testified that they were forced to abandon the strike in order to be able to pay the rent and feed their children.

On November 7, when the parties had just about reached agreement on terms of a contract which would have ended the strike, the company insisted that the union must agree to withdraw the fines before the company would sign the contract.

The trial examiner expressed sympathy with the company's position that the fines appeared to be excessive and might well inflict hardship on the six women. However, in a 1960 case the Board had held that a company committed an unfair labor practice when it insisted to point of impasse on including a contract clause limiting the union's authority to discipline or fine its members for exercising the right given them by the Labor Act to *refrain* from engaging in strikes. The Board said the subject of fines was not a mandatory subject of collective bargaining, that is, not a subject which a party could press to point of impasse (*Allan Bradley Company*, 127 NLRB No. 44).

In 1961 the Seventh Circuit Court refused to enforce the Board's order. It held that the subject of fines *was* a mandatory subject of bargaining which could be pressed to point of impasse (*Allan Bradley Company* v. *NLRB*, 286 F.2d 442).

It happened that the company's plant was located in Black River Falls, Wisconsin, which is within the jurisdiction of the Seventh Circuit. So, of course, the company had relied on the circuit court's statement of what the law was.

But in *Wisconsin Motors* (154 NLRB No. 1097), the NLRB said it did not acquiesce in the court's decision in *Allan Bradley*.

So the trial examiner stated that he was bound to follow the Board's view and therefore held that the company was violating the Labor Act when it insisted on a union agreement to drop the fines as a precondition of its executing the contract. And since, by so insisting, the employer prolonged the strike, he found that the continued insistence to point of impasse converted the strike into an unfair-labor-practice strike.

The trial examiner recommended that the Board order that

employees on strike on November 7, the date impasse was reached, be reinstated with back pay and that replacements hired during the strike should be dismissed, if necessary, to effect such reinstatement.

In seeking to differentiate its case from the *Allan Bradley* case, the company pointed out that it had made no demand for a clause in the contract covering the subject of union fines but had merely asked the union quietly to drop fines already levied. No denigration or loss of face would have been suffered by the union, the company stated.

The trial examiner thought it clear that the principle involved in *Allan Bradley* and in the case before him was the same. He added: "Suffice it to say that the violation herein found is predicated upon [the company's] insistence that a nonmandatory subject of collective bargaining be injected into the process of collective bargaining."

In this statement, of course, he was way off base. It was not the injection of a nonmandatory subject of bargaining into collective bargaining that the Supreme Court frowned on in the *Borg-Warner* case (356 U.S. 342). Parties are free to insist that a nonmandatory subject of collective bargaining be injected into the process of collective bargaining. It's the insistence to point of impasse that's illegal (*VOP Norplex Division of Universal Oil Products Co.,* Case 18-CA-2710 [1969]).

On June 29, 1971, the First Circuit Court at Boston handed down a startling decision on the issue of a union's right to fine strikebreakers.

That court, calling the case one of "first impression," refused to enforce a National Labor Relations Board decision that a Union violated Section 8(b)(1)(A) of the Labor Act when it sued 31 employees of a company in a state court to collect fines equal to the wages they earned during the strike. The employees had resigned from the union before crossing the picket line to return to work. *But they had voted to strike before the strike began.*

Section 8(b) provides in relevant part:

It shall be an unfair labor practice for a labor organization or its agents—

(1) to restrain or coerce (A) employees in the exercise of the rights guaranteed in section 7 of this title: *Provided,* That this paragraph shall not impair the right of a labor organization to prescribe its own rules with respect to the acquisition or retention of membership therein; . . .

Section 7 provides:

Employees shall have the right to self-organization, to form, join, or assist labor organizations, to bargain collectively through representatives of their own choosing, and to engage in other concerted activities for the purpose of collective bargaining or other mutual aid or protection, *and shall also have the right to refrain from any or all of such activities* except to the extent that such right may be affected by an agreement requiring membership in a labor organization as a condition of employment as authorized in section 8(a)(3) of this title. [Emphasis added.]

Section 8(a)(3) permits union shop contracts.

The decision is the climactic event of a strike which lasted from September, 1968 to March, 1970, unless, of course, the Supreme Court reverses.

The collective bargaining agreement between the company and union expired September 20, 1968. The membership voted to strike if no agreement had been reached by that date. The trial examiner found that "practically all the members" attended the strike-vote meeting and only one member dissented. A day or two after the strike began, the membership voted unanimously to levy a $2,000 fine on anyone aiding or abetting the company during the strike.

On November 5 and 25, 1968, respectively, employees Radziewicz and Kimball sent letters of resignation to the union. In both instances the union refused to accept the tendered resignations and warned the employees about the $2,000 fine. Radziewicz returned to work secretly for a few days before Thanksgiving but stopped working after receiving a second warning about the fine.

The two employees then filed unfair labor practice charges against the union on the ground that the threats of fines violated Section 8(b)(1)(A). The trial examiner ruled that no unfair labor practice had been committed. He added, however, that in his opinion, although *NLRB* v. *Allis-Chalmers Manufacturing Co.*, 388 U.S. 175, 65 LRRM 2449, established a union's right to obtain judicial enforcement of fines levied against members who cross a picket line, Radziewicz and Kimball could *not* be fined under *Allis-Chalmers* because they had effectively resigned from union membership.

The company thereupon informed all striking employees about the trial examiner's decision. The union, in turn, wrote to each member that the company's information was erroneous and that the union's right to fine strikebreakers has been upheld by the Supreme Court.

Beginning in June, 1969, twenty-nine additional employees resigned from the union and returned to work. The strike ended in March, 1970.

Each of the thirty-one employees who returned to work was tried at a union hearing and fined an amount equal to a day's pay for each day worked during the strike. All received notices regarding their hearings, but none attended and none paid the fine. The union then commenced actions to collect the fines in the New Hampshire state courts. While these actions were pending, the unfair labor practice charges resulting in the decision under discussion were filed. In conformance with his earlier opinion, the trial examiner ruled that, because these employees had effectively resigned from the union before crossing the picket line, the union fines and attempted judicial enforcement violated their Section 7 right to refrain from striking and constituted a Section 8(b)(1)(A) unfair labor practice. The Board affirmed his rulings, relying on its more extensive opinion in *Booster Lodge No. 405, IAM*, 185 NLRB No. 23, 75 LRRM 1004 (*Boeing*).

Here are points the unanimous court made in holding that the union did not violate the Act when it fined each of the 31 and sued to collect the fines in the state court. (The fines could aggregate $100,000.)

In the absence of an express provision to the contrary in a union's constitution or by-laws, they are to be interpreted as allowing voluntary resignations from membership *at any time*.

The union's practice of accepting resignations only during the annual ten-day "escape period," during which employees were allowed to revoke their "dues check-off" authorizations, did *not* bind the 31 members because they did not know of this practice and had never consented to this limitation on their right to resign.

But even if the resignation effectively severed ties with the union "for most purposes," the September, 1968 strike vote bound these employees to support this strike to the bitter end. Under the "charitable subscription" cases, a promise by A to donate funds to a charity is binding on A if others have made similar promises in reliance on A's promise. This principle is particularly compelling in a business context where donative intent is absent.

The court said this: "We suggest that this kind of mutual reliance is implicit in all strike votes; many employees would hesitate to forgo several weeks or months of pay if they knew their cohorts were free to cross the picket line at any time merely by resigning from the union. An alternative theory, also suggested by the subscription cases, is that the union can enforce an employee's agreement to strike since it has embarked on the strike in reliance on his promise to honor it."

An employee who agrees to strike should be likened to a volunteer for military service, who once he is enlisted, is no longer free to resign from his obligations and duties in midpassage.

The provisions in Section 7 of the Labor Act (quoted above) giving employees the right to "refrain" from striking, was not intended to authorize midstrike resignations. It merely gave them the right to refrain from joining the strike at its inception.

At the end of the opinion, the court backed away from the question: What about the guy who didn't attend the strike meeting? Can he resign in "midpassage"? It said in Footnote 8:

Since the record is somewhat equivocal on this point, it is conceivable that one or more employees will yet come to the Board with the claim that they did not attend either of the two strike vote meetings. We do not reach the question of whether employees in that position were free to abandon the strike at any time, whether their failure to resign at the beginning of the strike constituted ratification of the strike vote on their part, or whether their voluntary act in joining the union constituted with a "contract" as to bar such a claim [*NLRB* v. *Textile Workers Union of America,* 77 LRRM 2711].

This decision would seem to represent the biggest union victory since the Laidlaw decision. (That case held that a company has to go chasing after replaced economic strikers and offer them the jobs their replacements leave.)

Here are a few points to remember:

The NRLB will undoubtedly "respectfully decline" to follow the court's ruling. Thus for the time being it has effect only in the geographical area comprising the First Circuit (Maine, New Hampshire, Massachusetts, Rhode Island, and Puerto Rico). An order by the Board to rescind fines imposed on union members for voting to strike, then resigning and returning to work, won't be enforced by the First Circuit Court.

The First Circuit Court decision will have persuasive but not binding effect on the other circuit courts when considering whether to enforce a similar order.

The Board will petition the Supreme Court to review the First Circuit's decision. If that Court refuses to review, the other circuit courts are still not bound to follow the First Circuit's decision. A refusal to review means that four justices didn't think a review was required. It is not a ruling that the Circuit Court's decision states *the law.*

Does a strike vote bind a union member to strike to the bitter end if he wasn't at the meeting or voted against striking? Or does a majority vote to strike bind all members? Does there have to be a vote to fine members who return to work during the strike to bring the *Textile Workers* rule into play? The answers to these questions are still up in the air.

What about the amount of the fine? The Board held in the *Arrow Development* case, that it was *not* concerned with the size of union fines. It said the reasonableness of fines was up to local courts.

Companies facing a strike should let their employees know about this decision. Employees who don't want to strike should notify their union of that fact in writing. (An impractical suggestion, if ever there was one—few people want to be ostracized by their fellows.) If an employee votes "no" on a motion to go on strike, he should, if possible, have a witness to corroborate that fact (another impractical suggestion). How else is he to have evidence of exercising the "right to refrain"?

The unions are under a *duty* to inform their members of this decision before a strike vote is taken. If a union fails to do so, it will be found to have violated the Act. In the *Boeing* case (cited above) the trial examiner held that prior to or in the course of the strike, the union must issue a warning to employees not only about the possibility of a fine, but also indicate the amount or potential amount of the fine or the method by which it will be computed and the possibility of its enforcement in court.

If the Board petitions the Supreme Court to review this decision the petition will be granted. The vote in the 1967 *Allis-Chalmers* case in which the Supreme Court held that a union did *not* violate Section 8(b)(1)(A) when it imposed a "reasonable" fine on a member for refraining from participating in a strike and endeavoring to collect it by court action was 5 to 4.

Mr. Justice Black, joined by Justices Douglas, Harlan, and Stewart wrote a red-hot dissent. He said:

. . . The real reason for the Court's decision is its policy judgment that unions, especially weak ones, need the power to impose fines on strikebreakers and to enforce those fines in court. It is not enough, says the Court, that the unions have the power to expel those members who refuse to participate in a strike or who fail to pay fines imposed on them for such failure to participate; *it is essential that weak unions have the choice between expulsion and court-enforced fines, simply because the latter are more effective in the sense of being more punitive.* Though the entire mood of Congress in 1947 was to curtail the power of unions, as it had previously curtailed the power of employers, in order to equalize the power of the two, the Court is unwilling to believe that Congress intended to impair *"the usefulness of labor's cherished strike weapon."* I cannot agree with this conclusion or subscribe to the Court's unarticulated premise that the Court has power to add a new weapon to the union's economic arsenal whenever the Court believes that the union needs that weapon. That is a job for Congress, not the Court. (Emphasis added)

It takes four justices to grant a review of a circuit court decision. Justices Douglas, Stewart, Blackmun and the Chief Justice will vote to review.

If review is granted, the First Circuit decision will be reversed as the two Justices appointed to succeed the late Justice Black and ex-Judge Harlan will join the four named above.

19

HOW TO WIN BY USING THE LOCKOUT

ALTHOUGH IT WOULD appear that the employer's lockout is the corollary of the employee's right to strike, since the word "strike" in the Act is almost always followed by the words "or lockout," the NLRB until 1965 gave little protection to an employer when he closed his plant so as to bring economic pressure to bear on the union to accede to his demands.

In 1957 the Supreme Court approved a Board decision which held that a lockout was not a violation of the Act under the following circumstances.

The union bargained with a group of Buffalo linen-supply companies. It put into effect a "whipsaw" plan by striking only one company to gain its contract demands. (The "whipsaw" plan consists of knocking off the weakest member of the group first, then striking the next weakest member, etc., until the whole group has succumbed.) The rest of the companies shut their plants, thus locking out their employees. The union charged the companies with violating Section 8(a)(3) of the Act, which bans discrimination in regard to tenure of employment to discourage union membership. The NLRB found no violation because the lockout was "defensive" (*NLRB* v. *Truck Drivers*, Local 499 [Buffalo Linen Case] 358 U.S. 87).

Then in 1965 the Supreme Court held that in the Buffalo linen situation the unstruck members may lock out their employees and continue operations with temporary replacements (*NLRB* v. *Brown*, 380 U.S. 278).

On the same day the Supreme Court held that an employer—

167

a single employer, not a member of a multi-employer bargaining group—could resort to lockout as a means of bringing economic pressure to bear in support of his bargaining position after impasse had been reached (*American Shipbuilding Co.* v. *NLRB,* 380 U.S. 300).

The Court gave the Board a harsh reprimand, accusing it of trying to function "as an arbiter of the sort of economic weapons the parties can use in seeking to gain acceptance of their bargaining demands" and reminding it that Congress had not countenanced the Board's entrance into the substantive aspect of the bargaining process to this extent.

Thereafter, for about three years, the Board took the position that its former distinction between a "defensive" and an "offensive" lockout was dead. It held that a single employer did not have to wait until impasse before locking out if there had been extensive good-faith bargaining on all subjects and accord on many, but continuing disagreement on a work-assignment clause—and four years before there had been a crippling strike on this issue (*Darling & Co.,* 171 NLRB No. 95).

The Board even held that where a group of chain stores bargained as a group and one of the members had some nonunion stores, it could lock out the nonunion employees. The company did so because it thought such action was necessary to carry out the group's defensive lockout and to preserve the multi-employer bargaining unit (*Acme Markets, Inc.,* 156 NLRB No. 127).

But later, in *LaClede Gas Co.* (173 NLRB No. 35), the Board raised the possibility of the "defensive-offensive" distinction coming to life again. It condemned a selective layoff of employees without regard to seniority after an impasse had been reached on the ground that the layoff was not an "affirmative bargaining strategy" but was dictated by the employer's apprehension about a strike.

The law concerning what is and what is not a legal lockout is presently in a state of flux. The reason is that in the *American Shipbuilding* case the decision by the court and a concurring opinion by Mr. Justice Goldberg seemed to differ.

The facts in the case were recited by the court as these: "The company is primarily engaged in the repairing of ships, a highly seasonal business concentrated in the winter months when the freezing of the Great Lakes renders shipping impossible . . . Throughout the negotiations the employer displayed anxiety as to the union's strike plans, fearing that the unions would call a strike as soon as a ship entered the Chicago yard or delay negotiations into the winter to increase strike leverage."

These facts impelled Justice Goldberg to say in concurring with the majority's conclusion:

I reach this result not for the Court's reasons but because, from the facts revealed from the record, it is crystal clear that the employer's lockout here was justifiable. The very facts recited by the Court in its opinion show that this employer locked out his employees where, had the choice of timing been left solely to the unions, the employer and his customers would have been subject to economic injury over and beyond the loss of business normally incident to a strike upon the termination of the collective-bargaining agreement.

But this is what the Court said:

We hold that an employer violates neither Section 8(a)(1) [which forbids an employer to coerce employees in the exercise of their right to engage in collective activity] nor Section 8(a)(3) [which forbids an employer to discriminate in regard to tenure or other conditions of employment to discourage union membership] when, after a bargaining impasse has been reached, he temporarily shuts down his plant and lays off his employees for the sole purpose of bringing economic pressure to bear in support of his legitimate bargaining position.

How to win. Since the law on the subject is obviously in a state of flux, one is allowed to gamble. A company willing to take the loss inherent in shutting the plant in order to attain its contract objectives may bet on the continued validity of the statement from *American Shipbuilding* quoted above. If it guesses wrong it will have to face a back-pay penalty.

If a company wants to play it safe but still is tempted to use the lockout to attain its contract objective, it should forget the whole idea unless it can, many months later, prove that:

It always had a record of playing the game fair and square with the union.

It never discriminated against or discharged employees because they engaged in union activities or in order to discourage union membership activities or in order to discourage union membership (this is particularly important where lockout is contemplated in initial contract negotiations).

It had bargained before and after the lockout. Impasse had been reached (contrary, *Darling & Co.*, cited above).

Its motivation was not antiunion animosity.

It was faced with a situation of a threatened strike where, had the timing of the strike been left solely to the union, the company would have been subject to economic injury over and beyond the loss of business normally incident to a strike (the Goldberg opinion).

It didn't hire replacements during the lockout (*Inland Trucking Co.*, 179 NLRB No. 56—The *Brown* decision to the contrary notwithstanding, since that was a multi-employer case).

20

YOU MAY BUY A UNION CONTRACT AND
A UNION WHEN YOU BUY A BUSINESS

IN *William J. Burns International Detective Agency* (182 NLRB
No. 50), the NLRB decided that when one company buys all or
part of another company and continues its operations essentially
unchanged, it is a "successor" company and the predecessor company's union-contract obligations fall upon the successor company.

The union, of course, is also bound by the ruling and cannot
avail itself of the change in ownership to go after wage increases.

The obligation to bargain imposed on the successor-buyer includes the negative injunction to refrain from unilaterally changing working conditions without giving the union notice and an
opportunity to bargain about the decision to make such changes.
This is true even if the contract expired prior to the transfer of
title. This NLRB ruling resulted from a Supreme Court decision
in 1964 in which the court said that "a collective-bargaining agreement is not an ordinary contract" (*Wiley & Sons. v. Livingston*,
376 U.S. 543). In that case the court held that when a nonunionized
publishing company acquired a small unionized publishing company by merger, it had to submit grievances of the unionized
employees of the merged company to arbitration even though
it had not signed the contract with the union and, indeed, even
though the contract had expired.

The problem of just what is a "successor company" is causing
considerable litigation. A trial examiner has held that where
twenty-one employees out of a bargaining unit of 3,000 employees
were transferred to the company from an affiliated corporation
the company was not a successor bound by the collective-bargain-

ing agreement between the union and the former employer, here-after called the "predecessor."

The company and the predecessor were wholly owned subsid-iaries of General Telephone Company. Prior to 1967 the prede-cessor leased computer equipment from an outside firm. In 1967 the company was formed. It acquired title to the computer equip-ment. The equipment was transferred to a new building located two miles from the predecessor's operations as a telephone utility company. The twenty-one employees were transferred from the predecessor's payroll to the company payroll. The company en-gaged in furnishing data-processing services not only to the prede-cessor—its affiliate—but to outside companies.

The union demanded that the company be bound by its con-tract with the predecessor covering the twenty-one transferees as well as the other 2,979 employees still on the predecessor's payroll.

The trial examiner's principal reasons for holding that the company was not a successor were the small proportion of the unit involved, and the fact that whereas the predecessor oper-ated a telephone utility business, the company operated a data-processing business (*G. T. & E. Data Services Corporation,* Case 19-CA-4639 [1971]).

If you are about to buy a company or part of a company, you should follow these guidelines:

Consult with a labor relations lawyer before deciding on the amount of your offer.

Realize that a disclaimer of liability in the purchase contract has no effect.

Since you may have to arbitrate grievances which arose prior to the purchase, include in the purchase contract a covenant by the seller that they have all been revealed.

Since you may have to reinstate with back pay employees who have been illegally discharged by the seller, include a "hold harmless" clause in the purchase contract.

Watch out for restrictions on relocating in the seller's contract with the union. If the operation is to be relocated, consult with the union before making the final decision to relocate.

Remember, you "buy" the employees along with the business, so you will not be able to cut noncompetitive wage rates unilaterally.

If you too are unionized, try to get an agreement between the seller's union and yours on the vexing question of determining the seniority of your new employees. If possible, get an agreement to submit the problem to an arbitrator.

If you are the seller of a business you should:

Notify the union before signing the contract of sale and discuss possible effects on the employees of the change in ownership.

If union contract negotiations are being carried on simultaneously with the negotiations to sell, better bring in a representative of the buyer to sit in on the negotiations. You don't want to grant a 6 percent wage increase the day before the contract of sale is signed!

21

WHEN MAY A UNION HURT YOUR RETAIL STORE BY PICKETING OR HANDBILLING?

THERE IS A proviso at the end of Section 8(b)(4)—the anti-boycott section—which says that nothing in that section shall be construed to prohibit publicity, other than picketing, for the purpose of truthfully advising the public that a product or products are produced by an employer with whom the union has a dispute and are distributed by another employer.

It will be recalled that Section 8(b)(4)(B) says that a union may not induce a secondary employer's employees to strike or threaten verbally a secondary employer himself with the object of having him stop doing business with the primary employer, with whom the union has a dispute.

The Supreme Court has held that the word "produced" as used in the proviso is not to be taken literally. If the primary employer is a wholesaler, the union may picket retail stores only if the picket signs urge the public not to buy the specific products sold to the retail stores by the wholesaler (*NRLB* v. *Servette, Inc.,* 377 U.S. 46).

Similarly, it has been held that a television station is the "producer" of products advertised on its programs. A union can picket the advertisers so long as the picketing is aimed at the specific goods advertised. This is an application of a case known as the *Tree Fruits* case (377 U.S. 58). In that case the union had a dispute with Washington State apple packers who sold apples to the Safeway chain of retail stores. The union picketed Safeway after advising the employees not to strike and telling truck drivers to make the usual deliveries. The Supreme Court held that al-

175

though the Act prohibits consumer picketing aimed at all products handled by the neutral retailer, Congress did not intend to prohibit consumer picketing directed solely at a specific product of a primary employer.

Accordingly, it has been held that when a union both pickets and distributes handbills before a retail store, calling on the public to stop trading with the store because it advertises in a newspaper with which the union has a dispute, the union violates the Labor Act's secondary-boycott ban if the store's advertisements plugged *everything* the store sells rather than specific articles.

About nine unions struck the Los Angeles *Herald-Examiner*. White Front Stores advertised in that newspaper. Not a simple ad for Oleg Cassini originals or Hondas but a typical supermarket ad shooting the works: "Fantastic savings throughout the store!"

The unions picketed with sandwich-type signs urging the public not to buy goods advertised by White Front in the *Herald-Examiner*. They also distributed handbills carrying the same appeal.

A union may, however, engage in publicity other than picketing (i.e., handbilling) to urge the public not to buy any goods from a store which advertises in a paper with which the union has a dispute.

But a union may not picket to urge the public not to buy anything from the neutral store which advertises with the "producer" with which the union has a dispute.

Since the White Front advertisements advertised everything rather than a specific article or articles, the picketing was illegal even though the handbilling was legal (*White Front Stores, Inc.*, Case No. 21-CC-1116-1 [1970]).

22

HOW TO WITHDRAW FROM
A MULTI-EMPLOYER BARGAINING UNIT

IF YOU HAPPEN to be a small fellow in a multi-employer bargaining unit and you think the big boys in the group are being too generous, the Board has said that it will refuse to permit the withdrawal of an employer from a duly established multi-employer bargaining unit except upon adequate written notice given prior to the date set by the contract for modification or the agreed-upon date to begin the multi-employer negotiations: "Where actual bargaining negotiations based on the existing multi-employer unit have begun, we would not permit, except on mutual consent, an abandonment of the unit upon which each side has committed itself to the other, absent unusual circumstances" (*Retail Associates, Inc.*, 20 NLRB No. 388).

23

WHEN MUST YOU LET AN OUTSIDER DECIDE EMPLOYEE GRIEVANCES?

THE ANSWER IS this: when you have agreed to submit a particular grievance to an impartial third party—called an arbitrator—if you and the union can't settle the grievance by discussing it. That sounds like an easy rule to apply. But it isn't! For in formulating an arbitration clause in a contract it is impossible to reduce to writing the multitudinous grievances which can arise in the operation of a business. About the best you and the union can do is to agree in general terms that you will submit to an arbitrator any disputes concerning the interpretation or application of the contract which you cannot settle between yourselves.

Then, sure as shooting, a dispute will arise over a matter which you don't think requires any special interpretation of the contract. Or it will seem to you that you had reserved the right to do what gave rise to the grievance.

What can the union do?

It can get a court after you!

Section 301(a) of the Labor Act says that unions and companies can sue each other in federal district court for violation of a contract between them. The Supreme Court has held that this means that if a company refuses to live up to its agreement to submit disputes with the union to arbitration, the union can sue in the federal district court and the court will order the company to submit the dispute to an arbitrator for a final and binding decision. It also means that if the union has agreed to accept the decision of an arbitrator rather than strike to enforce its view of the dispute, the company may sue the union and the court will order the union not to strike (*Textile Workers Union* v. *Lincoln Mills,* 353 U.S. 448; *Boys Markets* v. *Retail Clerks,* 398 U.S. 235).

Suppose the union takes your company into the federal district court and asks the judge to order you to submit a particular dispute to arbitration—a dispute concerning contracting out work, for example. You don't think the company has agreed to arbitrate such a dispute, for although your contract with the union provides that differences between you and the union as to the meaning and application of the contract shall be submitted to arbitration, it also says that "matters which are strictly a function of management shall not be subject to arbitration." Surely this does not confide in an arbitrator the right to review your business judgment in contracting out work!

Or suppose it seems that nobody in his right mind could question the meaning of a clause. For example, suppose the contract says that on such and such a day the parties will meet "to discuss the payment of a bonus." But the union says these words mean "how much bonus shall be paid," even if that seems to be nonsense.

Or suppose an arbitrator issues a decision that seems clearly cockeyed? Prior to 1960, chances are the federal judge would have dismissed the case. But in that year the Supreme Court issued three decisions on the same day. They are known as the "Warrior Trilogy" from the name of one of the cases. In those cases the court made arbitration its special pet.

It held that if a contract calls for the arbitration of any and all disputes, then any and all disputes must be submitted to an arbitrator for decision. Thus it was up to an arbitrator to determine whether contracting out was "strictly a function of management." It was up to an arbitrator to decide whether "to discuss the payment of a bonus" might mean "how much bonus shall be paid." And it told the lower courts to enforce the awards of arbitrators even though they thought the awards to be clearly wrong.

Only if the contract said in plain English that such and such an issue was not subject to arbitration could a court refuse to order that a dispute be submitted to an arbitrator (*United Steel-*

workers v. *Warrior & Gulf Navigation Co.*, 363 U.S. 575; *United Steelworkers* v. *American Manufacturing Co.*, 363 U.S. 564; *United Steelworkers* v. *Empire Steel & Car Company*, 336 U.S. 93).

How to win. To beat the Warrior Trilogy you have to have enough economic muscle to get into your contract a "management rights" clause reserving to the company alone the right to decide what shall be done in almost every aspect of the business (for example, the sole right to determine whether to contract out work). You must also try to insert two clauses: a clause providing that the question whether the company has agreed to arbitrate disputes on any specific subject is for a court to decide, not an arbitrator; and a clause providing that if the company thinks an arbitrator's award exceeds the authority granted the arbitrator in the contract, the award must be confirmed by a court before the company may be forced to comply with it.

24

HOW TO PRESENT A CASE TO AN ARBITRATOR YOURSELF—AND WIN

ASSUME YOUR COMPANY has a contract with the union. It almost certainly will contain an arbitration clause. (For if it doesn't contain an arbitration clause it probably won't contain a "no strike" clause. And that will mean that whenever a dispute arises the employees can just walk out!)

Assume a dispute arises. The most common dispute is over the issue as to whether you fired or otherwise disciplined Joe Doakes for "just cause."

You aren't a lawyer. Do you dare present the case yourself to the arbitrator or must you hire a lawyer? That depends on the case. If Joe has socked a supervisor without provocation but nevertheless the union (perhaps motivated by internal political pressures) wants to carry the case to an arbitrator, the best lawyer in the world couldn't persuade an arbitrator to put Joe back on the payroll. But if the case involves an obviously difficult question of mixed fact and law, you take a big risk in presenting the case yourself. However, if your relations with the union are good and it intends to have its non-lawyer business agent present the case, you might well consider presenting the case yourself. The risk will be less if the arbitrator is a lawyer or a layman with a lot of arbitration experience.

How to win. To win an arbitration case you need five things: (1) a case you think you ought to win, (2) careful preparation, (3) effective presentation of the facts and arguments to the arbitrator, (4) the right arbitrator, and (5) a favorable submission agreement defining the issue. Let's consider each of these.

A good case. If after looking at the case from the union's point of view you aren't convinced that you have a good case and ought to win it, you should not present the case. You ought to settle it.

Preparation. Unless you prepare the case carefully you may very well lose it. First analyze the dispute and determine just what is the gut issue. Then interview each person (except the grievant) who witnessed the occasion that gave rise to the grievance. Cross-examine him to be sure you've got the whole story. Then reduce his story to writing and have him sign it. Check with other executives and with supervisors to determine if in the past a similar situation arose, and if so, how it was handled.

Be sure you know all the plant rules. Study the entire contract to determine if some other clause in it affects the clause at issue. For example, if the grievant has been disciplined for excessive absenteeism, quite obviously you can't hold against him his absence of three days to attend his grandmother's funeral if the contract contains a funeral-leave clause.

Try to figure out what your opponent will try to prove and see if you can scare up testimony that will rebut the testimony he will produce.

Prepare a trial brief. Put down on paper the points you must prove in their logical order leading to the conclusion you wish the arbitrator to reach. Then, under each heading, list the names of the witnesses who can testify to the facts needed to prove each point. Follow this outline in presenting your case.

Presentation. Sloppy or illogical presentation of a case can lose it for you. Remember, your job is to bring out the facts. Don't argue until all the facts are in.

Since you aren't a lawyer, skilled in the art of examination and cross-examination of witnesses, you might do just as well, after you have had him identify himself and his job, to ask the witness to tell the arbitrator just what he knows about the matter under dispute—not what he has heard someone else say about it, but what he himself saw, heard, smelled, felt, or tasted. Don't let your witness argue. That's your job. As for cross-examination of your opponent's witness the rule is *Don't,* unless you are absolutely sure what his answer will be, assuming he doesn't deliberately lie.

When you and your opponent have finished putting in the facts, ask for a five-minute recess and then, from the notes you have taken of the evidence offered by your and your opponent's witnesses, prepare a brief outline of an argument, which should lead to the conclusion you wish the arbitrator to reach.

If the case is at all complicated you may wish to ask the arbitrator for time in which to prepare and present him with a written memorandum or brief to refresh his recollection of the evidence and your argument when he sits down to write his opinion.

When the dispute involves the question of whether the company disciplined the grievant without just cause, the company should present its case first. In other disputes the union should go first. But it isn't worth raising Cain about. So long as all the facts are put before the arbitrator, it makes no practical difference who goes first.

Selecting the "right" arbitrator. An arbitrator is, of course, selected by some method agreed to in advance by the parties. They may select a specific individual to make an award in each dispute that arises. This individual should be honest, able, and impartial. Obviously, you aren't going to agree to the selection of the second cousin of the wife of the union's president. Nor is the union likely to agree to the selection of someone who has performed legal services for the company.

But there's more to it than obvious disqualifications. You don't want a fellow whose record shows that he's a "softie" in handling disciplinary cases—one whose attitude is always "Let's give him another chance" and who always reduces a discharge to a suspension. Nor do you want someone whose record indicates that he doesn't believe that management has the right to run the business except to the extent that it has not surrendered specific rights in the labor agreement—the right to contract out work, for example.

You can check an arbitrator's record by making a few telephone calls or reading some of his past opinions as published by the Bureau of National Affairs in *Labor Arbitration Reports*. The publication can be found in law libraries or in the public libraries of large cities. If the proposed arbitrator's past opinions are logically sound it is rather immaterial whether he has decided most cases for or against companies. If you have a good case you probably will win. A word of warning: beware the opinion of the loser in a case that the arbitrator was "lousy."

A second method of choosing an arbitrator is to provide specifically in the contract that a named individual shall decide all disputes arising under the contract.

A third method of choosing an arbitrator is to agree in the contract that the American Arbitration Association or the director of the Federal Mediation and Conciliation Service shall either name the arbitrator or furnish a list of five names from which each party will scratch two, leaving the fifth individual to serve as the arbitrator.

A fourth method is to have a three-man panel, each party naming its representative, who in turn choose a neutral third party. This, experience shows, is apt to be an unsatisfactory method of selection, as the two may not be able to agree on a neutral or, if they do, the neutral may fail to persuade one of the two to recede from the extreme view of the party he represents so that a majority opinion may be reached. Avoid it!

Negotiate a favorable submission agreement. A submission agreement is a statement signed by both parties which explicitly defines the issue in controversy and states what remedy the arbitrator is limited in imposing if he allows the grievance. The arbitrator is bound to conform to it. He has no authority to go beyond its terms. If he does, the losing party may go into court and have the award nullified.

Example: The undersigned hereby submit the following issue for final and binding decision to King Solomon: "To which woman does the baby belong?" If Solomon's award is that the baby be halved and one half given to each woman, he has exceeded his power.

Example: Is Jones entitled to the Electrician Class B rate? If the arbitrator awards Jones the Electrician Class A rate the award may be set aside. The issue should have been stated as: "To what rate is Jones entitled?"

Obviously, if you are more astute than your opponent when the submission is being drawn up, the arbitrator may have a tough time finding against you. Thus if the submission concerns whether the employees are entitled to an additional eight hours' pay when the plant is closed for vacation during the week that includes July 4, a paid holiday, the arbitrator cannot award them an extra eight hours' pay plus a day off.

Arbitration without an arbitrator. The Teamsters Union is an advocate of what is called the "open-end grievance procedure." Employee grievances are subject to final and binding decisions by a committee composed of an equal number of company and union representatives. There is no neutral or impartial member. The Board has approved this type of arbitration. Thus in *Terminal Transport* (185 NLRB No. 96) the arbitration board contained no neutral member. The grievant claimed he was discharged for refusing to withdraw a prior grievance filed by him. The company claimed he was fired for incompetency as a mechanic.

The panel issued the following decision: "The grievant is to be given the job of tearing down and rebuilding a 10-speed Road Ranger transmission in the presence of a union and company representative. The job is to be completed in the time prescribed in the flat-rate manual. If the employee properly completes the job and the transmission is operable, the employee is to be returned to work and paid for lost time. If not, the discharge is sustained."

Refusing to take such a test, the grievant attacked the procedure and reiterated his original complaint. The Board dismissed the complaint by a two-to-one decision. The "no neutral member" arbitration board was held to be proper. The dissenting member urged that the issue was not whether the company had a good reason for discharging the grievant but whether that was a mere pretext and the real reason was that he had too vigorously pursued a prior grievance.

Rules of evidence. If you've ever sat in on a trial you know that every now and then one of the lawyers will yell, "Object" and the judge will say, "Sustained." The judge is applying the rules of evidence, which have developed over the centuries because experience has taught that some types of evidence offered by the parties are not a trustworthy means of ascertaining the truth. The rules for the most part exclude evidence that is offered. Probably the most important one is that excluding "hearsay" evidence.

"Hearsay" is a statement by a witness quoting some other person concerning a matter which the court is trying to prove. It is objectionable because the party who is being quoted is not present and thus not subject to cross-examination. Suppose you are trying to prove that the grievant who was discharged had struck the foreman. The union puts on the stand a witness who testifies: "I heard Mike say that Pat didn't slug the foreman. He just called him a four-letter word." This is hearsay and should be objected to. The union should have put Mike on the stand.

However, unless evidence is totally irrelevant to the issue, most arbitrators take it over the objection of the other party "for what it is worth."

In one case a court set aside an arbitrator's award because he excluded evidence which had been offered because it was offered as rebuttal evidence rather than as part of the company's main defense. The court cited Rule 28 of the American Arbitration Association's rules, which reads in part as follows: "The Arbitrator shall be the judge of the relevancy and materiality of the evidence offered and conformity to legal rules of evidence shall not be necessary."

The court then quoted from Professor Benjamin Aaron of the University of California in his article "Some Procedural Problems in Arbitration," 10 Vanderbilt L.R. 743:

Despite the generally accepted principle that arbitration procedures are necessarily more informal than those in a court of law, objections to evidence on such grounds that it is hearsay, not the best evidence, or contrary to the parole evidence rule, are still frequently raised in arbitration. To the extent that these and similar objections are intended to exclude proffered evidence, they generally fail. The arbitrator is interested in gathering all the relevant facts he can, his principal objective is to render a viable decision, and any information that adds to his knowledge of the total situation will almost always be admitted.

Tips for Preparing an Arbitration Case

Read the entire contract to determine if any other clause in the contract modifies or otherwise affects the clause which allegedly has been violated and is the subject of the grievance.

Accept with caution any submission agreement defining the issue which is proffered by the other party.

Interview all supervisors to make sure a past practice in the plant does not in some way affect the grievance.

Consult your competitors to determine if a practice in the industry exists which may affect the grievance.

Cross-examine the grievant's immediate supervisor and all others on the management team to be sure you have all the facts which may affect the validity of the grievance. Be certain you know about any offers of settlement made during the steps of the grievance procedure and object if the union attempts to bring these out at the hearing. Offers of settlement are never admissible.

Obtain written statements from all witnesses and have them signed.

Read all past awards which may affect the present grievance and also dig out any settlements made during the steps of grievance procedures similar to the present one.

Figure out how you would represent the grievant to determine what arguments your opponent might make to shake your arguments.

Try to get the other side to stipulate as many facts as possible.

Know the history of the clause which is the subject of the grievance.

What to Do at the Hearing

If the grievance involves a disciplinary matter, the company should lead off; otherwise the union should.

Make a short statement saying what you intend to prove.

Object if the opposition's witness gives hearsay evidence—
"Jim told me that the foreman, etc." Suggest that Jim be called
to testify as to what he told the witness. But if the arbitrator
says, "I'll take it for what it's worth," keep quiet.

If the opposition tries to lead his own witness by saying,
"Isn't it true, Mr. Witness, that so and so happened," object. (But
he can lead your witness on cross-examination.)

Object if the union presents a statement from a witness who
could and should be present.

If a witness uses a word which is jargon of the industry, explain
it to the arbitrator. "Truck" may mean a handtruck, not a motor
truck.

Don't use six witnesses to prove the same fact. One is enough.

In disciplinary cases a stenographic transcript is worth the cost.

After the evidence is in, sum it up for the arbitrator and
make a short argument as to why he should find in your favor.

Needless to say, you should not communicate with the arbitrator after the hearing is over without the express consent of the
opposition. He's like a judge, and will resent any attempt to
influence him.